Our Buddy
Rescued for His Purpose

Bobbie Bruton

All scripture quoted is from the King James version of the Bible.

ISBN: 978-0692106112
ISBN-13: 0692106111

DEDICATION

I dedicate this book to the author and finisher of my faith,
my Savior and Lord, Jesus Christ; my husband and
children; and all who loved and were loved by
our beloved Buddy.

"All things were made by him; and without him
was not anything made."
John 1:3

CONTENTS

Bobbie Bruton

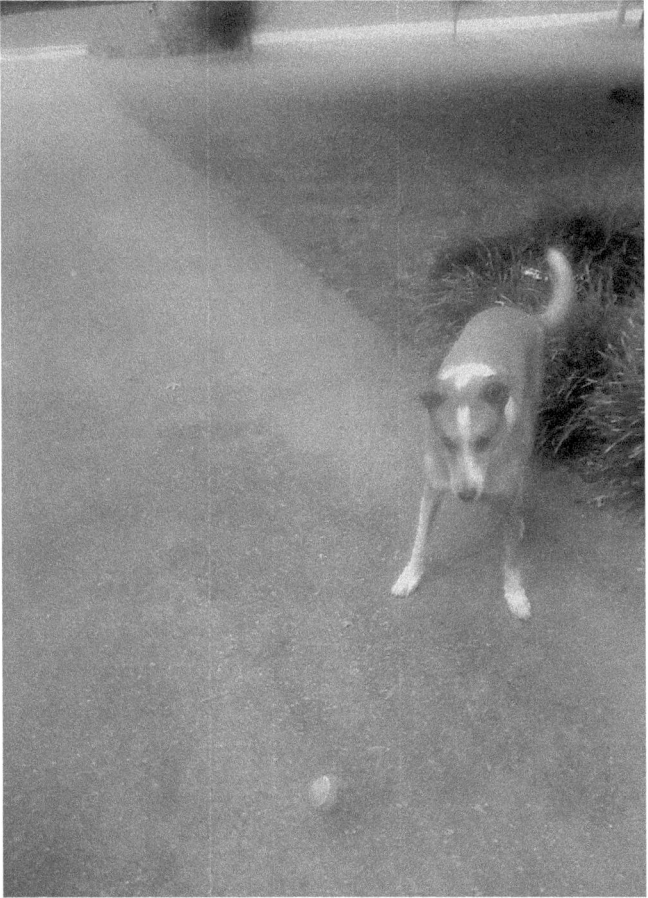

Buddy at six years old.

PREFACE

Love is our purpose. Why is it sometimes such a struggle to love and be loved? And why is it that dogs seem to have fewer struggles with love?

They share many of the same emotions as their human families: fear, jealousy, remorse, grief, loneliness, sadness, happiness, as well as anxieties. In addition, they share many of the admirable characteristics of their humans: bravery, devotion, loyalty.

For whatever reason, and without reading motivational books or attending classes or conferences to learn how to let go of hurts and offenses, dogs... just let it all go. They know how to love unconditionally.

Grateful for any attention or playtime, they learn to take in stride the comings and goings of their humans. They will drop their head at a scolding, and quickly forgetting and forgiving the reprimand and lack of attention, they will be waiting at the door with a smile and wagging tail, welcoming their human as though they had been gone a year, instead of an hour.

For me, it's one of life's mysteries that God chose to give dogs the ability and capacity to love so deeply and unconditionally.

Leave it to children to sum it all up. On social media, I saw a meme with this explanation from a six-year-old on the shortened lives of dogs:

"People are born so that they can learn how to live a good life. Like loving everybody all the time and being nice. Well, dogs already know how to do that, so they don't have to stay as long."

Although Buddy got along well with other dogs, he seemed to prefer humans for companionship and playmates. His love and relationships expanded far beyond the circle of his human family.

If ever a dog fulfilled its purpose to love, it was our Buddy.

ACKNOWLEDGMENTS

My gratitude and thanks must begin with the Creator of all that is seen and unseen, my Heavenly Father and Lord Jesus Christ. Thank you for creating canine creatures as part of the animal kingdom. And in your unfathomable design of all life, you granted these creatures the ability to love unconditionally.

To the unknown teenage boy, who was walking alongside a busy road on a cool spring morning, thank you for stopping at the sound of whimpering, coming from a ditch. Thank you for going down into that ditch and picking up a cold, frightened and hungry puppy. Thank you for rescuing that tiny puppy, thrown away to die, and taking him to the local shelter, giving him an opportunity to be adopted into a loving family.

Thank you to my husband, Steve, who has seen to the daily care of all our dogs. Thank you for keeping Buddy's food and water bowls full and giving him all his medications. It was you who also brushed his thick fur and bathed him ...when he would let you. Thank you for giving up the front planter to Buddy's lounging spot, instead of planting pansies there.

Thank you to our children, Seth and Betsy, who brought so much fun to Buddy's life, especially during his puppy years, allowing him to join in whatever sport you were playing around the house and sharing your friends with him. Thank you for giving him the perfect name, Buddy. And to my son-in-law, Lawrence, who helped me take Buddy to his last visits to our veterinarian, thank you.

Thank you to our wonderful neighbors, who not only welcomed Buddy into their yards but also into their hearts. All the times we left to go on trips, whether it was for a weekend, a few days or a couple of weeks, we knew Buddy was left in the best of care. Thank you for all the times you saved food from special meals for him. And thank you so much for all the belly rubs, hugs and kisses you gave to him. Most of all, thank you for treating Buddy like a member of your own family.

And to our veterinarian and his staff, we appreciate all the excellent care you have given to all our dogs over the years, including our beloved Buddy.

Our Buddy

1 WELCOME TO THE FAMILY

2003

∞∞∞

The sun was high in a nearly cloudless sky as we pulled out of our driveway, headed to a park about an hour away. It was a Saturday, and a perfect day for a picnic. And it was finally June, the month I had been dreading and eagerly awaiting since the past December. For the past six months, June had represented the beginning of known and unknown changes for our family.

It was in early December that my husband, Steve, had been told that the company he had worked for more than 20 years would be shutting down in June. It was in mid-December that I had attended an editorial meeting at my work to discuss and plan for a huge special section, commemorating the 100th anniversary of our local newspaper, that would be published the first week of June. This was in addition to two more special sections due to be published in May. This meant that in addition to my daily work and weekly deadlines, I would be conducting many interviews, writing stories, taking photos and planning for the layout and design for my contributions to these special sections. It was going to be a busy six months, but in June I would be on a lighter summer schedule and done with special sections for a while.

In early spring, our children had brought up the subject again of getting a dog. Our son, Seth, 12, and daughter Betsy, 9, both reminded their dad and me that we had promised to get them a dog. For several years, our neighbors' beautiful golden retriever had hung out at our house, playing with our children and their friends. I had told the kids that there was really no need for us to get a dog while they had the neighbors' dog to play with.

Running out of excuses, I realized that if our children were going to have a dog during their childhood, now was the time to get one. My husband and I promised to get them a dog after school dismissed for the summer. With his work ending in June, he would be home with them during the summer and could help them learn to take care of the dog.

Now that we had a time set for getting a dog, I began to think about the breed we should get. I had noticed another dog in our neighborhood that was about the size that I thought would fit our family. This dog was a Scottish Terrier. I began researching this breed and then looked for a rescue group. I found a rescue for Scotties right in our town. I talked to the kids about the Scottish Terrier breed and showed them pictures of the dogs on the rescue Website. They were both excited at the prospect of adopting one. After filling out an application online, I waited to hear from the director of the rescue.

A few days later, the rescue director called me. I told her we were looking for our first family dog. She wanted to know if we had a fenced-in yard, which we did. She also asked how long the dog would be alone during the day. At that time, she had three dogs in foster care, waiting for homes. The guidelines for placing these dogs were strict, and I wondered if she was going to approve us.

A week or so later, she called me back to tell me about an upcoming gathering of Scottie rescue groups from several states that would include a picnic near our area. She invited my family to the picnic for an opportunity to meet the dogs and the families who had rescued them. The picnic would be in June. Since my work schedule would be lighter then, I asked her if I could interview some of the rescue families for a feature story for the paper. She was very pleased with this request and quickly agreed to the story.

With my husband at the wheel of our van, I settled back in my seat and took out my notepad and jotted down some questions I planned to ask during my interviews at the picnic.

A week earlier, I had sent my section for the paper's centennial edition to press. Still tired from the long hours in completing the work on this section, as well as two other special sections that had been published in May, I was relieved to have all the stress from those additional deadlines behind me. Along with the exhaustion and relief, I also felt a sense of great accomplishment in my work.

When we reached the park, I was surprised at the number of cars already parked around the covered picnic shelters. I noticed many of the cars had out-of-state license plates. Followed by my husband

and children, I made my way toward the closest picnic shelter and then caught sight of the director of our local rescue. She came to greet us, and after I had introduced her to my family, she led us to the tables at the far end of the shelter. A tall dark-haired woman met us there, and I learned she was the director of the largest Scottie rescue group in our state. For a few minutes, we talked about her work in the city, which primarily involved rescuing puppies from puppy mills. It seemed as soon as one puppy mill was shut down, another one would be discovered. As we talked, there was a constant stream of beautiful Scotties of varying sizes walking by us, as their owners led them out to a grassy area.

A few minutes later, I made my way to a family sitting nearby and met their Scottie and listened to their rescue story. Many of the stories I heard were horrible, as I moved from table to table, interviewing families who had adopted Scotties that had been rescued from deplorable living conditions. It was amazing to see how the care and love of their adopted families had   transformed these abused and neglected animals into healthy and happy pets.

While I was conducting interviews, my family moved among the tables with me, and my daughter and I stopped to pet all the Scotties that came up to us. I noticed that when my husband and son would reach down and try to pet the dogs, they would shrink back. After this happened a few times, I mentioned it to the director who was accompanying me and introducing me around the shelter. She nodded her head and said, "Yes, Scotties will do that. Many times, they will attach to one or two people and ignore the rest of the family."

I looked over at my husband and son, who were now sitting at a table at the far end of the shelter, removed from the dogs and their families. Next to me, my daughter was taking delight in a Scottie that had stopped to nuzzle her outstretched hands. My heart went out to my son, who had been excited to come to this picnic and meet the dogs. None of these dogs had been friendly toward him and his dad. Not one. My son had waited a long time for the right time for us to get a dog. It wouldn't be right for us to get a dog that only attached to my daughter and me.

After I had concluded the interviews and finished taking pictures, I followed my family back to the car. The picnic had been fun and revealing. And I had reached a decision. As much as I liked the Scottish Terrier breed, it was not a good fit for our family. We needed a family dog — a dog that would love all our family.

As soon as we were in the car, I told my husband and children that I thought we should continue our search for a dog at our local animal shelter. They agreed. I still didn't know if we had or would be approved for adopting a Scottie, but now it didn't matter. Next Saturday, when we visited the animal shelter, most likely we would be leaving with a new family member.

***

It was Saturday again. Everyone was up early. We planned to be at the animal shelter as soon as it opened. I still needed to unpack and do laundry from our brief stay at the beach. We had left for the beach earlier in the week and had returned home the previous night. It was our first trip to 30A on the Florida Panhandle, and we had fallen in love with the beaches there. Although our stay was short, I felt rested and refreshed.

Unpacking and laundry would have to wait. We had a promise to keep. After visiting the shelter, we planned to take the kids to visit their grandparents, who lived a little more than an hour away.

As we drove up to the block building that housed the shelter, it appeared that we were the first to arrive. As we opened the door, we were greeted by a woman sitting in the office. She showed us to the room where the dogs were located. The kids split off from their dad and me and went to look at the dogs directly ahead. Steve and I turned to the right and stopped to look at an older dog.

As a family, we hadn't talked about an age range for a dog, but I think both Steve and I had in mind an older dog. Before we had time to move on and look at another dog, both kids came running over and said, excitedly, "We found our dog!"

"Are you sure?" I questioned them, wondering at this quick decision. "We just got here. You couldn't have looked at all of them."

"We don't have to look at all of them," my son declared. "We know he is the one, and his name is going to be Buddy."

We followed the kids back to an enclosure, holding a tiny brown and white puppy, now jumping in excitement at the return of the kids.

"Are you sure you want to care for a puppy?" I asked. Both kids nodded, "yes," so I went in search of the woman who had brought us to the canine room.

"We've found our dog," I told the shelter worker. "That didn't take long," she said, smiling at us.

"Which one is going home with you?"

The kids pointed to the puppy. She took him out of the enclosure and said she was going to take him to another worker who would bathe him, while we were attending the paper work.

As we followed her back to the office, she told us what she knew about the puppy. He had been at the shelter for about two weeks. A teen-age boy, walking alongside a busy road on the edge of town, had heard a whimpering sound in the ditch. Upon investigating the sound, he had found a tiny puppy and brought it to the animal shelter.

The worker said the puppy's weight was now at five pounds, and his age was approximately eight weeks. He was believed to be about six weeks old at the time he was found in the ditch. Of course, this guesstimate of his age could have a variance of one to two weeks, placing him older or younger. She thought he was a collie/terrier mix, pointing out that he had the ears of a terrier.

I was surprised at the amount of paperwork that went into an adoption, including a contract for us to sign. In addition to the adoption fee, we would be required to complete his vaccinations and pay for neutering. There was a schedule for all of this. We were given a complimentary bag of dog food and waited for the puppy to return from his bath.

Finally, we were on our way home with him. But first, we stopped and bought a collar, leash and dog house. The dog house looked big for a tiny puppy, but we knew he wouldn't stay little long.

After we arrived home, the kids took him into the fenced-in area of our backyard. Buddy was so excited as he ran around examining every corner of the fence. Then he squeezed himself through the wooden slats and was running on the other side of the fence. The kids ran after him and retrieved him and put him on a leash and let him discover the rest of the yard.

Steve hurriedly began putting together another fenced-in area for him near the garden, using the metal fencing around the garden that would contain him until he grew some and could safely stay inside the wooden fencing.

Buddy just kept smiling and smiling. I couldn't remember ever seeing a dog smile like Buddy was smiling. He seemed to know he was home, and it was evident he loved his new home.

While Steve worked on the fence, I took pictures of Buddy as he continued exploring the grass, trees and walkways, all part of his new domain. And he kept smiling. I sat him on top of his new dog house and snapped a picture. And he was still smiling. Smiling big.

After lunch, I put a laundry basket, lined with a towel, in the back seat of the van and told the kids to bring Buddy and put him in the basket for the trip to their grandparents. As my son brought Buddy to the open door of the van, I saw Buddy's smile fade. He protested as he was lifted down into the basket and tried to jump out. He didn't want to be in the van. His gaze was on the outside of the van. His yard. His home. And he didn't want to leave. But he did leave. This was the only trip Buddy ever took out of state, and it was only about 20 miles over the state line. This was his only "pleasure trip," although it's doubtful he considered it "pleasurable."

From that time on, Buddy only left the house for a vet visit. It was a struggle to get him in the van or truck for those visits. He was a homebody. He loved his home and didn't want to leave it. He would watch us get in the van and leave, but he never wanted to go with us.

***

When I picked up the ringing phone, I was surprised to hear the voice of the woman from the animal shelter on the other end. "What could she be calling about?" I wondered.

"It's time to make an appointment to have your puppy neutered," she said. "He will need to stay overnight at the vet's to be observed. They like to do these on Friday afternoon, and you can pick the puppy up on Saturday morning."

"He's only been with us for two weeks," I reminded her, feeling uneasy at the prospect of him spending a night away from us, so soon. More than a little anxious, I asked, "Isn't this something that can be done a few months from now?"

"No," she replied. "Your contract states that he is to be neutered before turning three months old. This needs to be done in the next two weeks."

"But he's so tiny," I protested. "He only weighed five pounds when we picked him up two weeks ago, and I'm sure he hasn't put on more than a pound, if that. Can we at least wait until he's little bigger? I will get him neutered. I would just feel better if he was a little larger and had a little more time with us, before we leave him overnight."

She insisted he had to be neutered right away. This conversation was annoying and frustrating to me. He was our dog, and we had paid a hefty adoption fee for him — almost half the amount required by the Scottie rescue group, which included up-to-date vaccines and neutering. We were also responsible for paying for all Buddy's vaccines. He had developed a cough his first week with us that required a vet visit and treatment for the cough.

We had been told to take him to a certain vet who worked with the shelter, who was supposed to discount his services.

Reluctantly, I agreed to schedule the surgery for the week before he turned or supposedly turned three months old, since his birthdate was unknown. But I sure wasn't happy about it. He was our dog now, a beloved member of our family, and I didn't like someone else making decisions for him, especially decisions that I didn't agree with. This was a part of adoption that I hadn't counted on.

***

It was Saturday morning, and we couldn't wait to pick Buddy up. I called the veterinary clinic to see what time we could come for him. The girl who took my call said he would probably be checked by the vet within an hour, and if all was well, he would be released to go home. An hour or so later, we got a call that Buddy was ready to leave.

As the kids and I walked into the veterinary clinic, it seemed like a week since we had seen Buddy. The night before, we had missed him so much and wondered how he was doing from the surgery. He was so little, and fearful thoughts plagued me all evening. We didn't know the time the surgery was done or how it went. I just hoped Buddy didn't feel abandoned by us.

While we waited for Buddy to be brought out, a woman working at the desk presented me with a bill for the surgery. When I looked at the bill to fill in the amount on my check, I almost gasped. This was more than the amount I was expecting to pay. I wondered how much it would have been if no discount had been applied. But all of that was forgotten when Buddy was brought out to us. He was wearing a red kerchief around his neck and looked adorable. But something was different about him. For the past four weeks Buddy had been living with us, his personality was very mellow. He was a happy and laid-back little fellow. Now, he seemed hyper and even a little hostile and aggressive. I wondered if some of the medication given to him had caused this change and if it was just temporary.

At home, Buddy seemed to cheer up and the hostility left. Over the weekend, his smile returned, and he seemed happy to be home. But as the days, weeks and months passed, that mellow personality we had observed during those four weeks prior to the surgery did not return. Instead, a hyper and slightly aggressive nature became part of his personality.

For the remainder of his life — even as he aged — he seemed to stay in a perpetual puppy phase. I was convinced then, and remained so through the years, that neutering him too early was responsible for that change.

A few days later, I called the animal shelter and reported that Buddy had been neutered. I asked if the charge to me was correct and was told that it was. I then asked what else had to be checked off the contract for us to fulfill our obligations. I was told that once all his vaccinations were completed, we would no longer be bound by a contract. I could not wait to be free of that contract. While we were having to follow their schedule and rules, it appeared Buddy still belonged to them.

Finally, Buddy's vaccinations were completed, and we switched to a vet we knew from church. Buddy was truly ours, now. We had no regrets about the financial obligations involved with Buddy's adoption. He was special. He was of intrinsic value to us and worth every hoop we had to jump for him.

~~~

2 PLAY BALL

2004

∞ ∞ ∞

I t was late afternoon on a mid-summer day as I slowly pulled into the driveway of our house, greeted by a familiar scene. On the right side of the driveway, a pile of bicycles rested on the grass, while their owners played softball on the other side. After I parked the van in the garage, I headed to the mailbox and noticed the kids had stopped their game and were discussing the rules — their rules.

Both my son and daughter were in the group, and it appeared the teams were comprised of all girls and all boys and one dog, Buddy, who was playing for both sides. As I walked back from the mailbox, I overheard one of the girls say, "Okay, we've got the rules set. Let's get to playing."

Amazed at how quickly they had worked out whatever disagreement had brought about their huddle, I couldn't help but think back to the years my son, at ages 5-8, had played organized tee ball and coach's pitch.

Almost every evening had been spent at the ball field, with no time for playing with neighborhood kids or doing much of anything as a family. Most of the time spent at the ball field was sitting on a bench and waiting...for hours.

About the only time I saw any real smiles on the kids' faces was at the end of a game, when they were given a free hot dog and soft drink. The kids didn't seem to care if they won or lost a game.

One evening my son forgot his glove, and as I was driving through our neighborhood to our house to retrieve it, I met two young boys riding their bicycles. The boys were pedaling slowly, seemingly without a care in the world. It was a picture of a child's idyllic summer's evening.

I thought about my son sitting back on a bench at the ball field with kids he did not know or go to school with. Sure, the kids on his team knew each other's names, positions played and usual batting order, but there was little opportunity to know much else.

It was just endless waiting during practices and games, along with watching some coaches and parents exhibit behavior more immature than the children they were coaching and parenting.

It wasn't even our son's favorite sport. He played his favorite sports during the school year with friends.

That summer, we decided that family activities would take precedence during the summer and ended organized ball activities. It was a decision that we never regretted. It was a decision that allowed our children to make memories with friends in their neighborhood.

When they were little, our kids played with the kids living in sight of our house. Once they were in school, they met other kids in our large subdivision.

Our house sat on a level corner lot, and that is where the neighborhood kids came to play. I was so thankful to have so many kids living near us, and that it was at our house they all gathered.

And even happier than I was at the sight of all these kids was the newest member of our family — Buddy.

As I walked back from the mailbox, I noticed that all the kids had retaken their positions. Up to bat now was my daughter. I watched as she swung at the ball. When the ball sailed past first base, she took off running, and Buddy ran with her. Stopping at first base momentarily, she headed for second base with Buddy right behind her. He waited with her until she made it to home plate.

As I continued watching, I observed that Buddy would run the bases with the other kids, as well. "Hmm, could it be Buddy is going to play sports like his namesake?" I wondered to myself.

When our son, Seth, had told us at the animal shelter, the puppy would be named Buddy, I didn't question him about this choice. After all, a lot of dogs were named Buddy.

But later at home, he told us he had named the puppy after the golden retriever in the movies that played sports. Well, that Buddy was in movies. Dogs in real life didn't play sports, did they? We found out that summer that our Buddy did. And it wasn't just softball.

On these long summer days, after finishing a game of softball, the kids would sprawl on the grass for a while with water or sports drinks and decide what to do next. If they ambled over to the trampoline for a while, Buddy would lie down next to it.

Sometimes, they would play street hockey. Other times, they would set up goals and bring out a ball for a game of soccer.

If the group was small, they would shoot around at the basketball goal. Buddy watched them and learned to bounce the ball with his nose. Whatever they played, if there was a ball involved, Buddy joined in.

Whenever Seth's friends would decide to play touch football, they would cross the street to the home of one of his friends and play in the friend's yard. Buddy would follow them and run after the ball. The guys just seemed to accept, as all the kids did, that Buddy was part of the team.

Of all the sports Buddy played with the kids, it seemed that soccer may have been his favorite. While the kids were in school, Buddy would find the soccer ball and bounce it in the air with his nose, much the same way he did with a basketball, and then run and retrieve it. When he tired of this, he would lay down in the grass with his paws folded over the ball.

During our second summer with Buddy we not only witnessed his skills in sports, but we also learned that he truly loved the presence of children of all ages and was sociable with other dogs in the neighborhood.

By the time he was a year old, Buddy weighed 50 pounds, double the weight the shelter veterinarian thought he would reach as an adult.

And it was during this time, Buddy began to take on the role of our protector. I often wondered during that first year if Buddy knew and understood that we had rescued him. With such a strong love for his home and us, Buddy could be trusted not to wander off. That summer, he began a "welcome home ritual" for us that continued for the rest of his life.

Whenever we returned home, regardless of the length of time we were gone, Buddy would meet our car in the driveway. When the car stopped, he would run to each side and look all around and then bark as if to say, "It's all clear. I've checked both sides of the car, and it's safe to get out. I'm watching over you."

It was as if he loved and appreciated us so much that he wanted to give back all he could to us, and most of all, protect us from any perceived harm. What loyalty! What devotion! And it started so early in his life with us.

~~~

Bobbie Bruton

3 RESCUED AGAIN

2005

∞∞∞

Sitting at the desk in the kitchen, in the late afternoon of a spring day, I hurriedly checked my email on the computer, and then turned my attention to a stack of mail lying under the computer monitor.

 It wasn't the time of month for the bills to come, so I flipped through the mail quickly, and then paused at an envelope from a Christian ministry I had been following for years. The letter inside announced the dates for an annual summer conference in California.

Capturing my attention and re-awakening a deep longing to finally, for the first time, attend one of these summer conferences, I thought, "Oh, how I wish I could go this year! But of all years, this year would be the most unlikely one to go."

Now into our second year with me as the primary breadwinner, I just didn't see how we could swing the trip. Apart from some temporary work and occasional consulting opportunities, Steve was still unemployed. When his company had announced it was closing two years ago, I knew we were starting a new faith journey but had not expected it to last this long.

Six months before the announcement, at the time we learned the company was in trouble, I had fasted and prayed the bank would work with the company, enabling all their plants to remain in operation and saving employees' jobs.

When the bank finally reached a decision that it would be working with the company, I was relieved and excited. And then, a few days later the company decided to reorganize and close two plants, one of which was the plant where Steve worked.

For days, I had thought my prayers had been answered. What happened? I prayed some more. I did not hear any audible words, but these words came clear to me in a way I can't really explain, except the words were there. "This is not a problem." That's all. Just that short sentence.

"How is Steve losing his job not a problem?" I wondered.

During the months the plant was preparing to shut down, we continued praying for another company to buy it. I specifically prayed a former owner of the plant would buy it. About two years after the plant closed, we learned the former owner had made an offer that was turned down. I didn't understand why this had transpired, but I remembered those words, "This is not a problem," and stayed hopeful.

Over the past two years, Steve had applied for many jobs and gone on a few interviews. At one point, he had an interview that was so promising it seemed certain the job would be offered. Although it would require relocating, we were willing to do that. But that, too, fizzled and came to nothing.

Learning to live on my salary, which was less than half of Steve's former salary, was just the beginning of financial restraints. Insurance that had been free through his work now took a big chunk of my check.

Despite our tight finances, I had been able to continue a savings deduction from my check that we had previously used for vacations and Christmas gifts for the family. My thinking was that I could always stop the deduction if needed, and the money already deducted was in a savings account. For the past two years, I had used this savings to pay extra on the loan on our van. Now our van was paid off, but I had continued to have the same amount deducted for savings.

Most days I didn't think about, and certainly didn't dwell on, the fact I rarely did any shopping anymore. We stopped buying fast food for the kids and ate most of our meals at home, except for pizza on Friday nights.

My gratitude ran deep that we had been able to make it this far on my small salary. Now that the van was paid for, we didn't have any debt. And more than that, I realized and was thankful the kids were getting extra time with their dad. Time for making memories they would one day cherish. They loved having him take them to school and pick them up in the afternoons.

Although I tried to focus on the positives, there were times I wearied of dashed hopes and disappointment after disappointment. I kept all these thoughts to myself, but there were days when I felt discouraged. Sometimes I felt like a hamster on a wheel, constantly spinning and accomplishing nothing. Sameness seemed to permeate my days. A trip to this long-awaited conference would provide a needed break.

As I took another look at the dates of the conference, I wondered how much a trip to California would cost for our family. Pulling up a discount travel site on my computer screen, I entered the dates for round trip airfare for two adults and two children. I was prompted to check if I wanted to include a hotel stay and ground transportation. I found a hotel next to the convention center where the conference would be held and checked it. I also checked round-trip shuttle service from the airport to the hotel and back. When the total appeared, I stared in disbelief.

***

"Buddy just about got hit," Steve announced, while walking into the kitchen.

"By the UPS truck?" I asked, with my eyes still on the computer screen.

"No, it was a car this time," Steve said, flatly.

"I don't know why he keeps chasing the school bus and UPS truck and now a car," I said, in exasperation, as I turned toward Steve, who had stopped to check on a dish he was making for supper.

"When it comes to everything else, he listens to us," I continued. "If we tell him to stop doing something, he stops. But when he heads for the road, he ignores us. And he just seems to be in the grips of hostility, while he is doing it. I still think he was neutered too young. He was very mellow and docile until he was neutered."

"What are you looking at on the computer?" Steve asked, turning his attention to me.

"Something I was curious about," I replied, looking back at the computer screen. "I was wondering how much it would cost for us to fly out to California.

"I would like to go to this conference this summer," I declared, as I handed him the letter with the conference information.

"More than we can afford," he said, dully, taking the letter.

"Here is the cost," I said, pointing to the bottom of the computer screen.

Looking at the dollar amount, and with a spark of interest in his voice, he asked, "That's just for airfare isn't it?"

"That's everything, including six nights in a hotel next to the convention center where the meeting will be held. It also includes shuttle service from the airport to the hotel. I couldn't believe it, either," I told him, with some excitement surfacing at his interest. "This same pricing came up yesterday when I checked, so I decided to run the airfares, hotel and shuttle transfers, again today. I still got the same prices."

"I'm still saving the same amount that we used the last two years to pay extra on the van. Now the van is paid off. Can we go?" I asked, hopefully.

"If we can all go for that price, then yes," he said, to my amazement.

I called the kids in and told them we were going to California. I showed them the available seats on the planes we were taking and let them choose their seats.

After the reservations had been processed, I called the hotel to make sure we were in their system. We were. Any remaining doubts about this deal were squelched when I checked with the airline and confirmed we were also in their system.

In utter amazement, I sat down at the kitchen table with a cup of coffee and reflected on what had just happened. All those years, even when I was still single, that I had wanted to attend this conference, and now I was going. Of all times, I would never have thought this would be the year to go.

"Mom, I can't believe we are going to California this summer," said my daughter, a little stunned herself, as she sat down next to me. "Daddy still doesn't have a job. I wouldn't have thought we could take a trip like this, right now."

"I know," I replied, in agreement. "This is a fantastic deal, and I receive it from the Lord."

"What about Buddy?" I asked, looking toward Steve. "We've never been away from Buddy that long. And who will take care of him."

"He won't care," said Steve. "He'll still be at home. I'll ask some of the neighbors to watch him and feed him, while we are gone. He already eats with the neighbors most of time, anyway. He'll be okay."

It was true that our neighbors did feed Buddy, regularly. Some days his food bowl went untouched. Not only had Buddy made friends with our children's friends, but he had endeared himself to the adults in our neighborhood, as well. Several families would save food from their meals for Buddy, and whenever they grilled out, they would feed him. At the time of our trip, he would be living with us two years and hopefully have a sense of permanence and not feel abandoned, I consoled myself.

***

As I was putting away laundry in the bedroom, I heard Buddy barking. He was in the fenced area near the garden that Steve had erected for him when he was a puppy. We still used it. It was also near the road, where he could see walkers passing by, giving him a change of scenery from the fenced-in backyard.

Looking out the window, I saw a tall, slim woman with long blonde hair pushing a stroller by our garden. She stopped at the fence and was talking to Buddy. She and her husband were our youngest neighbors at that time, and we were excited for them when they had a baby boy.

It had been several years since there had been a new baby in the neighborhood. I went out to greet her and see the baby.

Walking up to the stroller, I smiled down at the baby and glanced up at his mother, just as she handed a treat inside the fence to Buddy, who was smiling and wagging his tail at her.

"Buddy loves these peanut butter cookies," she said, matter-of-factly. "Every time he comes over to the house, I give him a cookie."

Surprised at this bit of information, I responded, "I didn't know he liked peanut butter or cookies. Where did you get those?"

"I buy them at the grocery. I keep them for my dog all the time. Buddy knows where I keep them and will go to the bag and bark for one, when he is at the house," she answered.

On my next trip to the grocery store, I picked up a bag of peanut butter cookies for Buddy. From then on, he always had a stash of cookies in the garage. And just as he would do at our neighbor's house, he would go to the bag and bark for a cookie.

***

 It was just past 7 o'clock and already dark when we pulled into our driveway on a Sunday evening in late October. When the garage door raised up and the light inside came on, we looked around for Buddy. It was still light outside when we had left around five that afternoon to go to our fellowship group from church. We had not put Buddy up, before we left. When he was outside, and we returned home, he always performed his ritual of barking and checking out both sides of the car, when it stopped. He did not meet us tonight.

Just as we started to search for him, we saw someone walking up our driveway. As he got closer, we recognized him as the husband of the young woman who had brought treats to Buddy. He told us that about an hour earlier Buddy had been hit by a car. He and his wife had picked him up out of the street and taken him inside their house. They thought his injury was limited to his leg.

When we heard that Buddy was unable to get up after being hit by the car, we knew that this young couple had saved him from a certain death from the next car that came along in the darkness of night. I think Buddy also knew he was rescued that night. Just as the teenage boy had rescued him from the ditch, and our family had rescued him from a kill shelter, this couple had saved him while he was lying in the road, unseen in the dark. Buddy already loved this family, and frequently went on walks with them, but from that time on he seemed to be on a mission to protect them, just as he tried to protect us.

Early the next morning Steve took Buddy to the veterinarian. After examining him, he didn't find any injuries other than his leg. After a week of rest, Buddy was able to walk again. When his leg was fully healed, he went back to running like a pup. Occasionally, we would notice a limp, but it was not a consistent limp and did not hinder him from continuing to race UPS drivers around the loop behind the house. No matter how much we scolded him, he would not stop. He seemed to enjoy the race. We tried to remember to keep him inside the fence when delivery trucks were out.

A few weeks before Buddy was injured, I was t-boned by a truck while driving our van. The policeman who worked the accident told me that only about an inch kept the collision from being very bad. The van was damaged but repairable.

My arm hit the steering wheel hard but amazingly was not broken. This was the second time the van had been hit by a truck while I was driving. For more than five years, the van had given us a comfortable and roomy ride. But with two collisions with large pick-up trucks, I didn't want to keep it any longer.

During the five weeks the van was in a repair shop, I prayed for direction about trading for another vehicle. I wasn't thinking about anything brand new.

A few days after we picked the van up from the body shop, we visited two dealerships in search of another vehicle. At one of the dealerships, we were offered half the amount we had originally paid for the van as a trade-in for a new SUV. It was an offer too good to pass up. Nothing had been farther from our thoughts that year than trading for a new vehicle. But we had one.

~~~

Our Buddy

4 ON GUARD

2006

∞ ∞ ∞

t was winter and a Saturday night. Steve's mother was now requiring home health care, and he was taking turns staying weekends with her. He and Betsy had left the day before, after school dismissal, to spend the weekend with her. Seth was at a friend's house. I was home alone but didn't really feel alone. Buddy was inside, just a few walls away from me. And I knew he was guarding me.

As I sat at my computer researching long distance train travel, I turned my head toward Buddy's abrupt and insistent barking. Getting up, I walked to the window and looked out.

As I adjusted my eyes to the darkness, I could see a figure moving on the driveway turnaround. Flipping on the porch light for a clearer view, I saw a deer scampering away.

Returning to my desk, I wondered how Buddy knew a deer was out there. Does he see and smell through walls? Did he somehow hear the silent steps of the deer? What kind of extra sensory abilities does he have?

Buddy continued to bark for a few minutes and for good measure even offered up a few growls. No trespassing was allowed on his watch.

For all of Buddy's affectionate and loving nature toward children, neighbors and other dogs, he did have another side. At times, he did exhibit another dimension to his demeanor.

When we adopted him as a puppy, we had no reason to think he would be anything but a spoiled pet. As mentioned earlier, for the first month that he lived with us, we had only seen a docile and mellow demeaner — until he was neutered.

The first time, I witnessed aggression from him was at a vet visit a few weeks after the neutering. One of the girls working the receptionist desk offered

Buddy a treat and then playfully took it back. But Buddy did not respond playfully to her.

Instead, he moved toward her with a low, menacing growl that I had never heard from him. She was taken aback and quickly gave him the treat.

That wasn't the last time I heard that growl, but it didn't happen often, and mostly it was at night when he heard deer or other animals in the yard.

When his low growl was directed at humans, it was usually delivery men, repairmen or other strangers. After we admonished him, he would quickly warm up to family and friends who were strangers to him. Although that low growl could spark fear in UPS drivers and mailmen, we never saw him try to attack anyone.

***

Buddy sat in the driveway and watched as we loaded suitcases, duffel bags and the kids' backpacks into the back of the car. We had about a six-hour drive ahead of us on the first leg of a trip that would take us back to California.

We planned to stay overnight with friends and continue driving to an Amtrak station the following day, where we would board a train for Los Angeles, and then onto Anaheim, the site of the Christian convention we were attending.

Our plane trip the year before had gone well. In addition to the convention meetings, we had enjoyed sightseeing and watching a baseball game at Angel's stadium. We had similar plans this year.

All of us were looking forward to riding the train and seeing more of the states we had flown over the previous year. One difference in this trip was that we would be gone two weeks.

Leaving Buddy for a week, the year before, had been hard. When he welcomed us home last year, I wondered if he was surprised and happy or just happy. My concern for him then and now was feeling abandoned by us.

The neighbor, who would be caring for Buddy, planned to let him stay outside for certain times during the day and put him up at night. At least his surroundings would be familiar, and he would see familiar faces.

***

We had just returned to our room from the complimentary breakfast served by the hotel, when Steve's cell phone rang. We had gone down to the dining room around 6 a.m. I wondered who was calling him so early. Then I remembered that California was on Pacific time.

I heard Steve tell his caller, "No, I'm not home. I'm in California."

After he hung up, Steve told me the call was from one of his former co-workers, who had heard someone was interested in buying and reopening their former workplace.

We had heard similar rumors before, and nothing came of them. No need to get our hopes up for this rumor.

Seth had also been on the phone with his friend, who lived across the street from us, and the friend said Buddy had been coming over every day and hanging out on his porch. That brought a smile to our faces.

***

Reflecting on our train trip, a few days after we had returned home, I came to a sudden realization that our trip almost ended the day it was to begin. Had it been left up to me, it would have ended.

When we had arrived at the train station, I checked with the security guard for parking information, as we had planned to leave our car at the station.

Although the train station offered free parking, the security guard seemed surprised we planned to leave our car there.

"There's no security here after 10 o'clock at night," she said, plainly. "This is not a safe area at night. I wouldn't leave my car here, all night."

"What about the parking garages nearby?" I asked. "Would it be better for us to park there?"

"You would have quite a hike carrying your luggage from the parking garage," she answered. "And if the train is late, and you arrive here in the middle of the night and call a taxi, the taxi might not even come. Taxis around here have been stiffed a lot by people calling them when they think their ride isn't coming, but then, their ride shows up before the taxi."

At this point I was about ready to call off the trip and head home. I did remember from my research that a shuttle service operated from the airport. I mentioned this to Steve, who did not want to cancel the trip. He was looking forward to the trip and thought we would be fine. But I knew from my research this train was often late and had the worst on-time record of any of the long-distance routes.

We headed out in search of the airport, found it without any difficulty, and then located the shuttle service. The owner of the shuttle assured us that he would be available to meet us at the train station, regardless of the hour we arrived on the return trip. He gave us his personal phone number to call when we were within an hour of arriving at the station.

All of us had enjoyed the trip and adventure of traveling by train. On the return trip, we had arrived back at the station in early afternoon, with the shuttle waiting for us.

Remembering how Steve was ready to continue with the trip, when I was overcome with fear, was a revealing moment for me.

For the three years following Steve's job loss, it seemed all the weaknesses of our relationship had been exposed. The trying times were not just about loss of income. Steve had lost his mother earlier in the year.

And role reversible had put a strain on our relationship, as well. Steve and I had both spent many years single as adults. We married later in life and had children later than most couples.

During the seven years I had been a stay-at-home mom, I had reverted to an overly submissive role, quite the opposite of who I was as an independent, single woman. For the first time in my adult life, I was dependent on someone else and this generated some dissonance.

Although we had some rental income from property I owned before my marriage, that money was deposited into a savings account. I still felt I wasn't contributing to the family, financially.

I was delighted and grateful to be able to stay home with my children and tried to overcompensate for my lack of income by not expecting any help with housework or the kids and unquestionably following Steve's decisions and wishes.

A loss of a job that Steve had held for nearly 25 years involved more than a loss of income: It was also a loss of identity and relationships with co-workers who had become like family.

While Steve was processing all this, I reverted to the independent woman I had been before my marriage. Steve had never dealt with any financial difficulties or hardships. But I had. I knew how to navigate through hard times. I had thrifty habits and could cut back on expenditures as needed. I knew how to hunker down in life.

Trying to be an independent married woman was different. Assuming responsibilities that were not mine began to feel like a crushing burden.

Wistfully, I looked back to the blissful blur of the years when I was a stay-at-home mom.

As I reflected over the past three years, I could see my husband and I had not been a team. Our weaknesses and strengths had not meshed. I knew about our weaknesses but what were our strengths?

Hmm...well for starters...I was good at starting, and Steve was good at finishing. I had tunnel vision and stayed on task. Steve was adept at multi-tasking. Our fears were different. When I was afraid, he wasn't. I saw the big picture, and he saw the details. I worried about the big things and didn't sweat the small stuff. He was concerned about the little things and didn't worry about the big stuff. I had a lot to think about.

~~~

5 NEW OLD FRIEND

2007

∞∞∞

As I sat in the car waiting on Steve, I looked at my watch and thought, "I will be so glad to get my interview over with and get out of these clothes."

Earlier that morning, I had seen my dermatologist in the city to determine the cause and treatment for the hives I had been experiencing for the past 11 days. For my doctor's appointment, I had dressed in the same clothes I planned to wear later in the day to an interview for a story I was working on.

It was a cold day in January, and I had worn stockings, along with a long skirt. Together, they were making the hives on my legs itch, almost unbearably, and it was still almost two hours until my interview was scheduled.

The dermatologist didn't know the cause of the hives and said to continue treating them with Benadryl.

Looking around the empty parking lot, I thought back to the times I had visited Steve at work and had to double park for lack of parking spaces. Today, only one other car was in the parking lot, and it was parked next to ours at the entrance to the building.

On our way back home from my doctor's visit, Steve had wanted to stop at his old workplace to see if there was any news about reopening the plant. No one here was expecting Steve. This visit was completely his idea and unannounced.

He wasn't gone long. As he slid behind the wheel, I noticed a somewhat dazed but happy expression on his face as he said, simply, "I start work on Monday."

"What!" I exclaimed in total surprise. I had assumed this visit was a follow-up to one of the rumors he had heard.

Still a little dazed, Steve told me the car sitting next to ours belonged to his former boss, who had just been contracted that week to restart the plant. Steve would be the second person back on the property. It was quite astounding for me to process this sudden news that Steve was returning to work.

In the weeks that followed, Steve worked on the physical restart, bringing back and setting up equipment, hiring contractors, electricians and security. He left early in the morning to go to the office, and after he returned home in the evenings, his phone continued to ring as he gave instructions to the new hires.

And he was loving it. I was more than a little in awe, as I listened to him take these calls. After nearly 25 years working at the same place, he knew his job and everyone else's. In fact, he knew this place like the back of his hand.

With everything happening so fast and Steve still technically a contract worker with no benefits, I kept to the same strict household budget I had been following for nearly four years. Before I typed up the first invoice for his pay, I opened a new checking account to deposit his checks. I just let those checks accumulate until he was offered a permanent position.

***

It was late afternoon on a sweltering day in early August, as I pulled into the driveway and parked next to Seth's car. It was still surreal that he was now 16 years old, had a driver's license and a car and was driving to school.

Once Steve had been offered and accepted a permanent position at work, my thoughts and worries had settled on the fact that our son would reach that anxiously awaited birthday in the spring that would allow him to obtain a driver's license.

During the months preceding his birthday, I had talked to the mothers of his friends who shared the same apprehensions about their sons driving —— driving alone without a parent in the car.

Most of the other parents said they wanted to buy their sons used cars that were practically junkers, in case they were in an accident.

My thinking was the opposite. I wanted my son driving a car with the latest safety features. After a lot of research, I found a car that offered the features I was interested in and was also an economical vehicle that should see him through college. It wasn't a cool car, but it was a new car. And it was now sitting in our driveway.

After saying "hello" to the kids, I told them I was home a little early, because I was going across the street to interview our neighbor for a feature story I was working on for the 30th anniversary of Elvis Presley's passing.

Upon meeting my neighbor, a woman around my age, when she had moved into the neighborhood about two years ago, I had learned that she was a huge Elvis fan and had won a national Elvis contest, as a teenager. Carrying my phone, notepad and a camera, I headed out the door and walked down the driveway.

As I knocked on my neighbor's door, I still hadn't noticed that I had been followed. After opening the door and welcoming me inside, my neighbor looked past me and exclaimed, "Oh there's my Buddy! Are you wanting a belly rub, Buddy?"

She brought Buddy into the living room, and after hugging him, began talking sweetly to him as she rubbed his belly.

More than a little surprised, I said, "I didn't realize you even knew Buddy's name, much less knew him." Of course, I was aware that Buddy was friends with many of the children and dogs in the neighborhood, as well as most of our surrounding neighbors, but I didn't know he was friends with her. In fact, he seemed to know this neighbor better than me.

Occasionally, I had stopped and had a conversation with her when we were both at our mailboxes. Passing by in the car, we waved, but that was pretty much the extent of our relationship. Buddy, it seemed, was on affectionate terms with her.

Turning back to me, she smiled and said, "Oh yes, Buddy comes and sees me all the time. He loves me, and I love him.

"When you all leave and Buddy's outside, he will come over here and stay while you all are gone," she continued. "We feed him, too. When we grill out, we always give Buddy something to eat, and I will save him something from supper if it's something he likes."

That wasn't a surprise. We knew neighbors had been feeding Buddy for years. We rarely gave him table food. Buddy frequently passed up the dog food we bought him for the neighbors' food.

With an Elvis CD playing in the background, Buddy stretched out on the floor and remained quietly, while we talked about the King of Rock and Roll.

~~~

6 DOUBLE TROUBLE

2008

∞∞∞

Following the sound of Buddy's incessant bark, I opened the garage door and yelled toward the driveway, "Buddy, come here!"

As always, he ignored me and continued barking and circling Seth's friend's car, stopping to gnaw at each tire. I couldn't figure it out. He loved Seth's friend. Why did he hate his car? Buddy did this every time this friend pulled into the driveway. Seth and his friend carpooled to school, and today, it was his friend's turn to drive. Buddy continued with the barking and gnawing until the car pulled away.

In some situations, Buddy could be compliant and obedient, and in others he just ignored commands and continued to do what he wanted to do.

For instance, if we wanted to put him up inside the fence, we only had to say, "Buddy, let's go inside the fence," and he would follow and go right inside the fence, without any prodding.

During the years before Buddy came to live with us, we had kept spring and fall flowers in a flower planter next to the front porch. This became a favorite spot for Buddy to conduct his guard duty, and no matter how many times we told him to move to the grass, he would not.

Buddy did not like being inside the house. He seemed to consider all the yard his domain. I think he really believed the planter belonged to him, and he could rest there whenever he wanted.

As the children in the neighborhood grew up, and some moved away, he spent less time playing with small children. Most of his dog friends had now passed away.

Seth and his friends still included Buddy when they played basketball and football.

One of the highlights of Buddy's day was taking a walk with the young couple, who lived across the street, and their son. As soon as Buddy would see them leave their garage, he would be racing toward them to join them on their walk. Usually, the couple would stop momentarily to let their son pet Buddy. Then Buddy would trot off with them, smiling with every step.

**

Leaving the snack bar, I walked carefully through the coach cars of the train we were traveling on, carrying two paper cups of coffee. Behind me, Seth followed carrying soft drinks and snacks.

As I approached our seats in the back of the last car, I noticed a bewildered look on Steve's face. Sitting in the seat next to him was our daughter, who had tears streaming down her face.

What was going on? Seth took the window seat across the aisle, and I sat down next to him and looked across at Steve, who was holding his phone in his hand.

Did he just get an emergency call? Was it his dad?

"What's wrong?" I asked him, anxiously.

"I just got a call from the secretary at work. The company is declaring bankruptcy and shutting down," he said in a monotone voice, with a stunned expression on his face.

"When are they shutting down?" I asked, suddenly feeling numb, trying to absorb this news.

"Today. This afternoon. They told all the other employees this afternoon that today is their last day. Since I was on vacation, they called me, just now, to tell me," he answered, his voice flat and still in disbelief at what he had just heard.

"How can they do this in just one day? When they shut down before, you had six months' notice," I reminded him.

Another thought hit me. "Will there be a severance package?" I asked, hopefully.

He shook his head, "No."

I sat back in the seat and sipped my coffee. I didn't want to say too much in front of the kids.

We were on the last leg of the return trip on a train that had taken us up the Atlantic Seaboard, starting from Savannah, Georgia, and ending in Portland, Maine. It was about 4:30 in the afternoon, and we would be on the train all night, arriving back in Savannah around 6:30 a.m. the next day.

As the news about Steve's job sunk in, I felt scared — more like terrified. What would we do?

How did this happen? I looked over at Steve and asked, "Did you have any inkling about this?"

"No," he whispered, through tight lips.

That was strange. Steve's perception about situations was usually spot on. I knew that he hadn't agreed with the overspending by some new hires in management. About six months after the start-up, he had settled back into his former position and was just working out of that department.

Steve's former boss was no longer there, and his position and other management positions had been filled by people with little to no knowledge of the product. The operation had still not reached the previous company's level of production when it had shut down. Still, there had been no indication that the current company was in danger of financial collapse.

As the train clicked along through the night, and the sound of falling rain joined the hum of the tracks, my thoughts ran ahead to the coming day, the coming weeks and the coming months. This job loss was going to be different. Not only was there no preparation or severance package, but now, I didn't have a job, either.

Earlier in the year, I had taken a medical leave for some health problems and near the end of the leave found out I would need surgery. At that point, I had decided to give up my job.

Shortly before we had left on this trip, I had been released from the doctor and had been looking for part-time work. Now I would be looking for full-time employment.

As soon as we returned home, I found a full-time job that interested me and applied for it. Immediately, I was contacted, and an interview was scheduled.

***

As I waited in an outer office to be called back for an interview, a woman working at a desk nearby began a conversation about the fall weather. She mentioned the upcoming anniversary of the passing of a family member.

Trying to hold back tears and explaining the ones already falling, I said, brokenly, "My brother passed away one week ago, today. I still can't believe he is gone."

She got up and came over and hugged me.

The day after we had returned home from the train trip, the same day I had applied for this job, my brother, David, was admitted to the hospital with a reoccurrence of an illness that had nearly taken his life, more than five years prior to this crisis.

For a week, I had spent every day at the hospital. At first, he recognized me and other family members but gradually slipped into unconsciousness. Then he was gone.

With grief still so fresh and raw, I tried to compose myself in preparation for the interview. I needed this job.

A few minutes later, I was called back for the interview. Before I left, I knew the job was mine.

~ ~ ~

7 NEW ADDITION

2009

∞∞∞∞

I t was a sunny Saturday morning in early November as we made the short drive from our house to pick up Betsy's puppy. Just a few days before, I had been sitting in the high school parking lot waiting for school dismissal, when I got a call from a woman Betsy had contacted through an ad, who had a litter of Labrador retriever puppies for sale.

For at least a year, we had checked ads looking to rehome a lab, but each time we were too late, and the dog had already been placed.

These puppies were the offspring of AKC parents and were reasonably priced. Betsy had asked for one of the puppies for her Christmas present.

When I told the woman on the phone about Betsy's long search for a lab and this would be her Christmas present, she asked if I could bring her to her home that night to choose one from the litter.

"We have four yellow and nine chocolate puppies," she said. "As of now, only one female chocolate is reserved. She can have her pick from the others."

We set up a time that evening for the visit, and when she gave me directions to her house, I was surprised to learn that she lived within two miles of us.

I couldn't wait to give Betsy the news when she got to the car. We were both excited that after all this time, she was finally getting a lab and, except for one puppy, would have her pick of the litter.

That night she picked out a chocolate male. He was almost old enough to leave but needed a vet visit and shots.

Earlier this morning, the call came that we could pick him up. As we turned into the drive leading to the house, we saw a quilt on the grass with the whole litter squirming in the sun. It was an adorable sight to see.

After parking the car, we walked over to the quilt. Some of the puppies were sprawled on sleeping siblings.

When the owner joined us, Betsy found her puppy among the sleeping ones. The owner told us the puppy had just been seen by the vet and weighed five pounds. That was Buddy's weight when we brought him home with us.

The owner gave us a small stack of papers that included forms for AKC registration and the puppy's birth information and family history. We had never seen Buddy's parents and litter mates and could only guess his mixed breeds. We didn't know his birthday or where he was born.

At home, I read the puppy's family history, which was impressive, and then put away all the papers in a drawer, including the AKC registration papers. Registering him would not increase his value to us or make us love him more.

***

If the puppy had been registered, he would have been named Sawyer Bentley, but since his papers were never mailed, he was called Bentley. He was introduced to Buddy as his new brother.

Buddy smiled at him and looked slightly amused at this little ball of fur that wanted to investigate everything in his path. This was quite a change from the laidback and barely moving bundle Betsy had taken from the quilt.

At bedtime, he was not showing any signs of tiredness or sleepiness. Betsy had planned for him to sleep in her room, but when she put him in his bed, he began whining. The whining gave way to crying. We took turns trying to comfort him, assuming he was missing his mother and siblings. Finally, he fell asleep — briefly. This continued for most of the night. He would sleep for a few minutes and wake up crying.

This pattern of wakeful sleeping repeated the next night. I didn't know what to do for him. As a pup, Buddy had never done this. During some research online, I learned that putting a ticking clock or another dog next to a pup would remind it of the comfort and reassurance of its mother. I didn't have a clock that ticked, but I did have another dog.

I put Bentley's bed next to Buddy's bed, and the crying stopped. He slept through the night next to Buddy. That's where Bentley wanted to be, next to Buddy. And that's where he continued to sleep.

***

Watching Bentley go through his puppy phase was entertaining for us and brought many smiles. We hadn't had much to smile about the past year. Steve was still unemployed. Due to the recession, his extensive job search had only yielded one phone interview. A lay-off at my new workplace included me. With both of us unemployed, it was a scary time, a trying time. Somehow, we made it through.

One day, as I was thinking about our situation and comparing our current job losses to Steve's previous job loss, I realized our relationship was much better this go-round. We were supportive of each other, and our home was not out of order. I was not trying to lead the family, as I had previously.

This was a time of leaning heavily on our faith and trusting the Lord with our circumstances and with what we knew and didn't know about all the "whys" of our situation. During this time, I thought about the stability of Steve's workplace during the early years of our marriage. It had been confirmed the owners during those years had made an offer to take back ownership before the first shutdown, and that offer had been refused. I began praying this company would make another offer that would reclaim ownership and provide a stable work environment.

In addition to our job losses and the struggles with our job searches, we had both lost family members. A few months after my brother's death, Steve's dad was hospitalized several times, never fully regaining his strength. He had passed away about three months ago.

Yes, Bentley and his cute puppy ways brought smiles, daily. Even Buddy seemed to enjoy watching Bentley and his antics.

***

Watching from the back door, I saw Buddy go into his dog house that was still inside the backyard fence. He rarely used it anymore, unless he was inside the fence during a rain storm. I pushed the record button on my phone just as Bentley walked over to the entrance to the dog house and began barking loudly for Buddy to come out.

I wondered what Buddy would do. Buddy still considered all the yard and everything in it as belonging to him, and he certainly knew the dog house belonged to him. With an air of entitlement, Bentley kept his stance and continued barking. To my surprise, Buddy emerged from the dog house and allowed Bentley to take his place.

I was fully expecting Buddy to put this pup in its place. Watching Buddy's gentleness and patience with Bentley revealed another layer of his temperament I hadn't seen before. Everyone who knew Buddy found something to love about him. Bentley was no different. In the coming months, it was evident that Buddy had become a hero to Bentley.

~~~

8 GOOD BROTHER

2010

∞∞∞∞

Hearing a series of yelps coming from the patio, I hurried to the back door to see if Bentley was in trouble. He was in a dilemma of his own making. Now three months old and weighing 25 pounds, he had managed to jump onto a patio chair and then onto the table. Now he was afraid to jump down.

It was a touching and hilarious scene that I had to film first, and then I helped him down and brushed some snow off his beautiful brown fur. It was January, and our first measurable snow had fallen the night before. Earlier that morning, I had taken Bentley outside to see his first snowfall. His brother and babysitter, Buddy, lay nearby looking quizzically at Bentley.

As I started to go back inside, I stopped at the door and looked back. Bentley was back on the table. He looked at me and began yelping, again. Walking back to the table, I tried to coax him down onto the chair, but he made no effort to jump even that slight distance. He kept looking at the ground and then back at me. I helped him down, again. This time I turned the chairs over, so he couldn't get back onto the table.

By this time, Buddy was rolling around in the snow-covered grass. Forgetting about the fun of climbing onto a table, Bentley joined him and together they enjoyed making snow angels.

As I watched the two of them, I couldn't help thinking how differently they had gone through the puppy stage. I had never seen Buddy show any kind of fear, and as sociable as he was, he was also content by himself. Bentley didn't like to be alone and seemed timid in many situations.

I was glad Bentley had Buddy. He still slept next to Buddy and followed him constantly when they were outside. Buddy didn't seem to mind. I wondered if Buddy was noticing Bentley's growing body. Although he still exhibited puppy behavior, he was catching up quickly with Buddy in size.

***

Sitting at my computer on a June morning, I was searching a national employment site for a certain position — Steve's old job. There it was. It was posted.

About a month ago, we had learned Steve's former workplace had been bought by a company that had previously owned it. This was the company I had prayed would make another offer. It was exciting news. During the years Steve had worked under their ownership, the work environment was stable and well managed.

As I looked at the ad for the position Steve had held prior to the first shutdown and after the restart, I noticed a few changes in requirements and responsibilities. A master's degree in the field was now required. Steve had done some post grad work but didn't have a master's degree.

Certification in a certain computer program was also listed. This reminded me of some contention I had had with Steve during the first shutdown. Almost a year after the shutdown, I learned his severance package included tuition to complete this very computer program now listed as a requirement for his old position. Unknown to me at the time, he had turned down the tuition and opportunity.

By the time I found out about it, the enrollment period had passed. I had encouraged him to enroll in the course and pay the tuition himself. With so much going on, I had forgotten to nag him about it, and he never enrolled.

During the restart, this computer program had been available to Steve but was not required or often used. Steve had worked more than 25 years without it and didn't need the information to do his job. Although he didn't have certification in the computer program, he did know the basics and had some working knowledge of it. But still, these new requirements had me wondering how much emphasis would be placed on the computer knowledge versus experience.

Before Steve had a chance to apply, he was contacted by a headhunter to see if he had any interest in the position. Around the same time, two of his former bosses contacted him to make sure he knew about this newest restart, and both wrote letters of recommendation for him.

And then we waited to hear from the company. We waited and waited and heard nothing. We did hear that several of his former co-workers were back at work. Steve's former bosses called to see if he was back at work. When he told them, he hadn't heard anything from the headhunter or from the company, they couldn't figure it out, either.

In the days that followed, Steve was frequently contacted by his former co-workers, who had returned to work and were unable to find the product as directed by the software. Steve didn't need the software and could point these workers to the right location over the phone.

I suggested he quit giving them free consulting. If they needed information, they could at least bring him on as a paid consultant.

***

It was Friday and mid-morning on one of those sunny, cloudless days in late October, when Steve came to me and said, "Bentley hasn't come back."

Part of Steve's early morning routine was to take Bentley on a four-mile walk. After the walk, he would let Bentley have 30 minutes of freedom to visit his doggie friends in the neighborhood, before returning him to the fenced-in part of our backyard.

This was concerning. Bentley did not roam freely around the neighborhood, except during his brief escapes from the fence, and even then, he stayed on our street. Buddy followed along as we walked down the street calling for Bentley. Seeing no sign of him, we drove around the other streets in the subdivision looking for him

Steve remembered seeing heavy traffic that morning, heading to the construction site of a new house near the end of our street. Maybe Bentley had gone there and was hanging out with the workers. We drove there and asked a worker if a dog had been hanging around. He said he hadn't seen a dog. It appeared that most of the workers were gone to lunch, so we concluded that he still could have been there at some point.

It was getting dark when the workers passed the house, leaving for the day. Now the day was gone, and Bentley was still missing. We went back to the construction site and called for Bentley, with no response.

Now, I was worried. Although it had been a warm and beautiful day, a weather system was moving in overnight, bringing rain and cooler temperatures. With heavy hearts, we returned home. Once more, we walked around the yard, calling his name, in hopes he might have come home while we were out looking for him. As usual, Buddy had met us and followed us around the house.

Later in the evening, the rain began falling. We could hear it on the roof. Betsy and I cried together, as we visualized Bentley wandering lost and scared in the rain and sleeping without shelter, while cold and wet. It was too much to even think about. I had never prayed for a dog and didn't know if God heard prayers for dogs, but I decided at that moment to pray for Bentley.

I asked God to keep Bentley safe through the night and give him shelter from the weather. I prayed that kind people would give Bentley food and water and ease his fears. And I asked God to bring Bentley home to us.

The next morning, I made calls to homes at the end of our street, asking if Bentley had been seen. No one had seen him. I called the office of our vet, which was about a mile away, and told them Bentley was missing and asked if anyone had reported finding him. No one had reported him.

We left our neighborhood and drove through adjoining subdivisions, looking diligently for any sighting of him. We extended our search two miles from the house. Each time we came home, we hoped to see Bentley waiting for us.

The next day, Sunday, a new thought came to me. What if Bentley was at the construction site and somehow went unnoticed inside the house.

Was the house locked up? Could Bentley be locked up inside the house? We knew the woman building the house lived in another house in our neighborhood. She was friends with our neighbors across the street. I called those neighbors and got her phone number.

When I reached the woman and explained why I was calling, she said she had caught a glimpse of a dog late Friday afternoon as she was arriving to check on the new house.

"It was almost dark, and I couldn't see it well enough to identify it, but I did see a dog go around the back of the house," she said, assuredly.

"Then he couldn't have gotten into your house after you left, because you would have locked it?" I asked, wonderingly.

"The house isn't locked, and some areas are still open," she replied. "Maybe he found a way in and went up the steps and is afraid to come down."

"When he was a pup, he was afraid of heights," I told her. "Do you mind if I go out to your house and check the upstairs?"

"Not at all. Let me know if you find him," she said, kindly.

Steve and I, along with the kids, searched the whole house, calling for Bentley. But he wasn't there. I called the owner of the house and thanked her for allowing us to search for him.

Before heading home, we drove through the adjoining subdivisions for a second look, with still no sighting of him.

I researched lost dogs online and learned they rarely travel farther than two miles from home. It was suggested that after placing ads for the lost dog to check with all the veterinary practices in your city to see if a dog had been dropped off.

What if Bentley was stolen? He was such a beautiful dog and still intact. What a horrible thought that he might have been taken for a puppy mill. He had just turned a year old, and we were waiting to neuter him, following his first birthday.

Later that night, Betsy and I checked our online ad for responses. There were none. We read some of the other ads for lost dogs. They were heart wrenching. Some of the dogs had been gone for weeks.

The next morning, I found a list of veterinarians in the phone book and made the first call. While I was talking to the vet, call waiting beeped and my vet's phone number appeared on caller ID. When I took the call, our vet's assistant told me, "Bentley has been found. I have a number for you to call, and you'll be given directions to where to pick him up."

"How do you know it's Bentley?" I asked.

"We know it's Bentley," she said, "The caller had his tag number, and we verified it."

That was news to me. Steve took care of the dogs' vet visits, and I had no idea the tags on their collars had our vet's phone number and a number identifying each dog.

Immediately after hanging up, I called the number she had given me. The man who answered my call was our insurance agent, who lived about two miles from us. We had driven by his house twice over the weekend. He said Bentley came to his garage door around dusk Friday evening and was wet. This was before the rain moved in, and he thought Bentley had crossed a creek nearby. He had put food and water out, but Bentley was too timid to come near him. But he did come back for the food and water. Our agent also alerted his neighbors that Bentley was lost and might show up at their houses.

Several of his neighbors put food and water out for him, too. It was only this morning that Bentley had gotten close enough to him that he could read his tag number. I couldn't stop saying, "Thank you, thank you," for all the care Bentley had received from him and his neighbors. As soon as Bentley saw me drive up, he ran toward the car. As I opened the door for him, he gave me a sheepish look that seemed to say, "I'm sorry."

After all we had been through over the weekend, we decided to make an appointment with our vet, so that Bentley would not be desirable to a puppy mill. Maybe, it would help settle him down, and he would stay inside the fence.

When we picked Bentley up at the vet's, he showed no signs that the neutering had affected him at all. Nothing changed in his behavior and habits, and he did not settle down.

Buddy and Bentley

9 NEW BROTHER

2011

∞∞∞

Clutching a navy folder in my right hand, I waited anxiously to hear my name called. It had been almost a year since I had taken a test that qualified me to be here for this job interview.

During the past two years, I had applied for hundreds of jobs, but this was the only request for an interview. Ten positions were available, and I hoped to be offered one of them.

A few minutes later, I was called back to the interviewer's office. When I handed her the navy folder with my resume inside, she glanced at it and put it aside. Something wasn't right. I had conducted hundreds of interviews for stories, while I was working in journalism and was accustomed to the basic process. This woman showed no interest in me and had few questions to ask. I began to suspect this was a fake interview.

I had applied for this position before there was an opening but had been told an expansion of services would include adding several positions. In addition, I had traveled nearly 100 miles to take a required test that took about four hours. When I received my test results, I had only missed two of the 95 questions. Although these were all entry level positions with a modest salary, benefits and insurance were included. My family really needed the insurance. After the Cobra from my last job ran out, we could only afford the catastrophic plans.

With my test results, work history and transferable skills, I felt that I was a strong candidate for one of these positions. Maybe, naively, I thought my qualifications would take precedence over my age. During the recession of the past two years, I knew that ageism had crept into the hiring process of the workforce. Younger people could find jobs, but older people were having a tough time just getting an interview.

Protocol dictated I had to be interviewed because of my high score on the test, but clearly, I was just being checked off the roster of applicants. At the end of the interview, I was told I would be contacted within two weeks if I was among those selected, and if not, I would be receiving a letter informing me of the hiring decision.

During the eight years Steve and I had been grappling with all the challenges of job losses and extended unemployment, I had, for the most part, remained hopeful and in faith, expecting a better future.

When I left that office, on the first Monday in January, I felt utterly defeated. I had no hope left. Week after week and month after month, I had sent out applications and resumes for jobs in my field, as well as for any jobs that I could apply transferable skills or that required only basic skills. When I was turned down for all of those, I still held hope for the position for which I had tested.

For the next three days, I cried and cried more. I cried during the day, and I cried at night. When I awoke on the fourth morning, a plan was unfolding before me. It's hard to describe how I became aware of this plan. It was just there in my thoughts as I was awakening, along with all the details. I went to my computer and started working on a spread sheet.

First, I listed all our resources, including my retirement account. Yes, I was going to retire.

During the years, I had paid into my account, I rarely thought about it. I wasn't planning to retire. What was the point of retiring, except to travel? I never had an end date in mind for working. Neither did Steve. Both of us were either borderline or full-fledged workaholics.

On this spreadsheet, I carefully entered all our expenses, month by month, for the whole year. I didn't leave anything out. I included dog food and medications and vet bills. I dug out utility bills and averaged those. I wanted all the numbers to be as exact as possible. After it was completed, I printed a copy of it and presented it to my husband.

"I'm done with applications and resumes," I told him. "As of now, I'm retired."

For the first time in two years, I did not spend the week searching for jobs and filling out applications and submitting resumes. It felt great. It felt even better the next week.

And since it was January and tax time, I made an appointment with the CPA who had been preparing our taxes for the past few years. When I went to meet with her, I took a copy of the spread sheet and showed it to her.

"What do you think of this?" I asked, after I had explained why I had made it. "Do you think it will work for us?"

After looking over it, carefully, she raised her head and smiled at me, "It looks good to me. I think you have a plan."

***

Peering through the blinds in the bedroom window, I could see the animal control truck backed up in a neighbor's driveway, next to our garden spot and the fenced-in area Steve had constructed years ago for Buddy. The animal control officer had turned the motor off the truck and was just sitting there and watching Bentley inside the fence.

A few days before, this officer had knocked at our door and told us a woman in the front part of the subdivision had reported Bentley roaming in front of her house. Because of Bentley's size, she said she feared for her small dog. The officer told us if Bentley was found on the loose again, we would be paying a hefty fine. Steve told the officer that Bentley stayed inside the fence, except when he took him on walks. The officer said this visit was a warning and next time, we would be fined.

Since the previous summer, Bentley had broken out of the fence several times. When he wasn't gnawing on the fence posts, he was looking for a way to escape. Although he weighed about 90 pounds now, he didn't appear tall enough to jump a four-foot fence. But he had jumped over it. Steve reworked the fenced-in area near the garden, making it taller and hoped it would contain Bentley. But somehow, he managed to break out of it, too.

One of our neighbors talked to the woman who had reported Bentley and told her Bentley was not an aggressive dog. He was just a big baby. She was unrelenting and assured our neighbor she would report Bentley if she saw him loose again.

It was unfathomable to me that another dog owner would send someone else's beloved pet to the shelter. It seemed to me that she was putting her small dog in more danger by letting it run loose in a large neighborhood with high traffic. Cars were a greater danger to her dog than Bentley would ever be.

As I peered out the window, I hoped Bentley would not get excited at the sight of the animal control truck and try to break out in front of the officer. Since Bentley had been reported, this officer was making daily visits to our street. We lived in a large county. Did this officer not have any other responsibilities and could just spend large blocks of time stalking Bentley?

This had become a worrisome problem for us that went beyond an occasional event to day-to-day concern. I didn't want Bentley to spend one hour at the shelter. We didn't know what else to do. We couldn't afford to have another fence built to try and contain him.

The long walks Steve and Bentley took around the neighborhood didn't seem to wear off any of his energy. Bentley hated being inside, but that was our last recourse to protect him from the animal control officer. It was heart-wrenching to see him confined day after day. The thought kept coming back to me, "Are we doing what is best for Bentley?" It was the middle of March. Is this the way he will spend the summer? It didn't seem right. We could confine him and see him every day, but what kind of existence was that for him.

Finally, I had a talk with Steve. "Do you think it would be better for Bentley if we found him a new home, where he could roam and play in water?" I asked him. "I just hate seeing him cooped up all the time."

"Well, we know he likes to roam and play in water," he said. "No matter how many times I work on the fence, he manages to get out of it. Neutering didn't slow him down."

We agreed to pray about rehoming Bentley. Gaining some confidence in praying for a dog since Bentley's lost weekend, I prayed for a kind and caring person to love Bentley and give him a home with water nearby and lots of land to roam, without fear of animal control.

A few days later, Steve received a call from a former co-worker and friend, who told him he had moved to a small farm with a creek and a pond.

"That would be perfect for Bentley," I thought. Steve had known this man for nearly 30 years. He was a recent widower and a kindhearted soul. He would be good to Bentley.

"Do you think he would be interested in taking Bentley?" I asked Steve.

"I don't know," Steve replied, thoughtfully. "I'll ask him when I talk to him again. He's supposed to be coming here to pick up some plants I'm giving him."

When his friend called back to set up a time to come for the plants, Steve asked him if he would be interested in taking Bentley. He said he would think about it. A few days later, he called back and said he wanted Bentley and would pick him up the same day he came for the plants.

***

Keeping a close watch on the time, I hurriedly finished my errands in town and headed back to the house. I wanted to be there when Bentley left.

Steve's friend was supposed to be at the house at 1 o'clock. When I pulled into the driveway, his truck was parked there. As I got out of the car, I saw Steve and his friend in the backyard, pulling up the plants.

When I got the garage, I saw Bentley sitting in his crate. He was shaking and had peed in his crate. Bentley never had accidents. He knew something was up, and he was scared.

As I cleaned his crate, I talked to him. "Bentley, don't be scared. You are going to a place where you will have freedom to roam, and you will have water to play in. You are going to have a creek and a pond to play in. This man, who is taking you to your new home, is a good man. He will be kind to you. Bentley, we are not mad at you. That's not why you are leaving. We love you, so much. We could keep you here cooped up all the time and see you every day, but what kind of life is that for you? It's going to be sad, at first, but you will love your new home. We are going to miss you, so much, but we will come see you. We love you, Bentley."

I can't say Bentley understood a word I said, but he did calm down. We walked to the truck with him and said, "good bye." I asked Steve's friend to please let us know if it didn't work out, and we would take him back. I told him we didn't want Bentley going to anyone we didn't know.

Lying in front of the garage, Buddy quietly studied our faces. Did Buddy have any understanding of what was going on? Did he know his brother was leaving and would not be coming back? Out of all of us, I think Bentley was attached to Buddy the most.

In the days that followed, Steve and I were swathed with sadness, questioning if we had made the right decision.

"Maybe we should have tried to have a taller fence built around the backyard," Steve pondered, sadly, knowing as well as I did, that we didn't have the money to build such a fence.

When Steve called to check on him, two days later, his friend told him Bentley was staying close to the house, so far. He said he was letting Bentley out for periods of time to get used to his place, when he could keep close watch on him. For the first week, he planned to keep Bentley put up most of time, in case he tried to run off.

We were relieved to hear that. I had not considered that Bentley might try to run away. Steve continued to call twice a week to check on him.

As it turned out, Bentley was adjusting to his new home, so Steve's friend only kept him contained a few days. He said Bentley had made friends with some other dogs down the road, but he always came back to the house. It was comforting to get these reports, but we still missed him, terribly. Sometimes, Steve and I would go on a short drive to try and relieve the sadness. We could see that Buddy had a tinge of sadness, as well.

One person who was not sharing in our grief was our daughter. Although Bentley was originally her Christmas present, she had never bonded with him. For the first few weeks, she would hold him and play with him and try to get him to sleep in her room. He never attached to her. He would scramble away, and at night, he always wanted to be near Buddy.

A few times, she tried to take him for a walk. After he pulled on the leash and dragged her down on the road, she gave up walking him, and eventually, her dad took on all the care for him.

Bentley had only been gone three weeks, when she told us she had found an ad for another dog that she wanted for her birthday. Steve and I were still grieving over Bentley and thought it was much too soon to bring home another dog. She kept begging her dad to go see this dog.

"This is a little dog. You won't have to worry about him getting out of the fence, because he will stay in the house all the time," she told her dad. "The puppy is a purebred Yorkie, but they don't have papers on him, so the price is lowered."

Steve gave in and said we would go see the dog, but he wasn't promising to buy the dog for her. Reluctantly, I called and made an appointment with the owners.

***

On the way to see the puppy, Betsy told us she had a name picked out for him. "I'm going to name him, Orson. The name means 'little bear,' and he looked like a little bear in the picture I saw of him."

Steve and I didn't like the name and tried to get her to consider a name more commonly used for dogs, but she was determined to name him, Orson.

After letting us into their house, a middle-aged couple introduced themselves as the owners of the father of the puppy. Their married daughter was the owner of the puppy's mother and would be arriving shortly, they told us. The tiny puppy looked like a clone of its black and gold father and was enjoying a game of chase with him. The father was young, only a year and a half, and small, weighing just four pounds.

At one point, the husband grabbed the puppy and put it up to his chest. It was apparent he had grown attached to it and wanted a few moments with it before he left. The wife told us the puppy was three months old and weighed two pounds. He was the firstborn of the litter of three and the smallest. His brother and sister had already left for their new homes. Because he was the runt of the litter, they had kept him longer to ensure he was healthy. The puppy had been born on Steve's birthday. If Steve had any reservations left about getting the puppy, I think they all left when he found out the puppy shared his birthday.

When the puppy's mother arrived, she was dressed in a cute outfit. Her full and lustrous coat was a silky silver and blonde mix. The puppy had inherited his mother's doll face.

As we were leaving, the couple gave us the puppy's toys and told us what he liked to eat. I could tell it was hard for them to see him go. I told them they were welcome to stop and see him whenever they were out our way.

Arriving home, we showed the puppy to Buddy. He smiled and wagged his tail but looked at him as if to say, "What are you? You don't look like a dog, and you don't look like the squirrels I chase." I'm not sure Buddy ever figured out what Orson was, but he didn't seem to consider him a dog.

Remembering how Bentley had cried his first two nights with us, I wondered what we were in for the first night with Orson, who had spent twice as much time with his parents than Bentley had with his parents and siblings. Surprisingly, Orson had a good first night and every night thereafter. There was no adjustment period with him. He was contented and happy with us.

ORSON

10 TO THE RESCUE

2012

∞∞∞

A s I turned onto our street, I saw Buddy resting on our neighbor's front porch. As soon as he saw me, he was up and running across the street. After he had completed his usual routine of checking both sides of the stopped car and giving me the "all clear" to get out of the car, he headed to our front porch and returned with a small package between his teeth.

For years, Buddy had been calling our attention to packages delivered while we were gone. If the package was small, he would bring it to us. When the package was too large for him to carry, he would tug at us and guide us to the porch.

Buddy seemed to have a special affinity with the UPS truck. Several minutes before it ever appeared on the hill in front of the house, he was barking in anticipation. As soon as the truck was in sight, he began the race around the loop, which included a steep hill behind our house, and concluded back on our street. When the truck was back on our street, Buddy would lie down again and watch it depart over the hill. For reasons known only to Buddy, this race was a huge thrill to him.

Once during a delivery, I apologized to the UPS driver about Buddy racing his truck, telling him we tried to keep Buddy inside the fence during delivery hours but sometimes forgot.

"Buddy is alright," he said. "We get along just fine."

"How did you know his name is Buddy?" I asked.

"Oh, I've heard you and your husband calling his name, when you've tried to get him back in the yard. I always watch for him when I'm going around the hill," he said.

That was a relief to hear, especially since Buddy had already been hit by a car.

The package Buddy had brought to me, today, contained a book our daughter had ordered for one of her college classes. She had finished all her high school work in December, a half-year early, and was now enrolled in the winter semester of college. Both our kids were now in college.

After presenting me with the package, Buddy nudged me to his cookie bag in the garage. I gave him two cookies. Steve always gave him one cookie, saying we had no idea how many more cookies or treats he was getting from the neighbors.

As he walked away to eat his cookies, I noticed he was limping again. Steve and the kids joked that he only limped around me to get sympathy for more cookies. "I hardly ever see him limping," Steve chuckled.

I wasn't so sure about that. Although he was now almost nine years old and still acted like a pup, he had moved into the senior years. I looked online for an orthopedic bed for him and found one with good reviews.

Buddy loved his new bed. For the first few days, after it arrived, he would hardly leave it.

* * *

After I had put away all the groceries from my shopping trip, I walked past the door to the garage on my way to the laundry room and noticed the door was ajar.

"Uh oh, where's Orson?" an alarm sounded in my thoughts, as I suddenly realized his absence. Usually, he was right under my feet, following every step I took.

"Look for Orson in the house," I shouted to my daughter. "The garage door is open, and I'm looking outside."

Running through the garage, I saw no sign of Orson in the driveway or front yard.

As I started to check the yards of the neighbors, a car came up the hill and as it drove by me, I flagged the driver down and asked, "Did you see a Yorkie as you started up the hill? My dog is missing." The driver said he hadn't seen a Yorkie.

Frantically looking about and trying to decide where to look next, I saw Buddy coming up the hill — walking in the ditch. That was strange. I went to meet him.

With a huge sigh of relief, I saw Orson taking slow steps in the ditch, hemmed in by Buddy, who wouldn't let him move toward the road.

"Oh, Buddy!" I cried out. "You kept Orson safe! You are my hero!"

Scooping up Orson, I gave Buddy a hug and exclaimed, "You are getting extra cookies, today!"

Sensing he had just performed an incredible deed in my eyes, and smiling that beautiful "Buddy smile," he followed me into the garage. Without counting, I grabbed a handful of cookies and put them in his bowl. "You just did a wonderful thing, Buddy," I said, smiling at him. "You saved your brother. Thank you."

***

It was a sunny Sunday afternoon in October, as we drove to visit Bentley for the first time, since he had been rehomed. The week before, I had celebrated my birthday without a call or birthday wish from my sister, Gaile. It was now six months since her sudden death, and still, it didn't seem real that she was gone. We were two years apart in age, and all my earliest memories included her. I missed her so much. Her birthday was ten days before mine, so both our birthdays this year were tinged with sadness for me.

After church, we had decided on the spur-of-the-moment to visit Bentley. Thoughts of seeing him again cheered me up.

Although he had been gone now for 16 months, Bentley still held a special place in our hearts. Steve still made weekly calls to check on him. From these calls, we learned that Bentley had adjusted to farm life and was happy.

During the early months Bentley lived on the farm, Steve's friend often remarked that Bentley wasn't bonding with him. He was friendly enough toward him, but that was all.

Steve told him that Bentley had not bonded with any of us, either. He did seem to like us, but he never welcomed us home the way Buddy did. He was not affectionate with us, nor did he respond to our affection for him. He did seem to care for Buddy, and I believe he did have a bond with him.

During Bentley's first summer on the farm, Steve's friend would take him along when he went to work on a house he was remodeling for his granddaughter. When he finished work, Bentley would hop back into the truck and return home with him.

When the granddaughter, a young school teacher in her twenties, moved into the house, Bentley met her for the first time. And he refused to get into the truck to go home with Steve's friend. He wanted to stay with the granddaughter and her two dogs.

"I cannot get him in the truck, anymore," lamented Steve's friend. "My granddaughter loves dogs, and she said he could stay. He loves her."

For about a year now, Bentley had been living with the granddaughter. Steve's friend was going to accompany us to her house. As we neared his house, I lost my cell phone signal and couldn't call him, so Steve guessed at which driveway belonged to him. It was the right one. The road to his house was two roads off the state road. I thought his road was way out in the country, until we turned onto the road his granddaughter lived on. Her road was nothing more than a lane, just wide enough for one car.

"Bentley sure doesn't have to worry about animal control stalking him out here," I thought to myself.

And then, we were parked in front of the granddaughter's house. Running to meet us was Bentley, who was still wearing the red collar we had bought for him. We opened both car doors on one side, and Bentley jumped from one door to the other, receiving our hugs.

Just as we were delighting in the fact he remembered us, he suddenly stepped away from the car and looked at us, as if to say, "I'm glad to see you all again, but why are you here?"

Standing off to the side were the granddaughter's other two dogs: a black lab and a large mixed breed. Bentley ran toward both dogs, and together, they all ran down the hill toward the creek. When he reached the bottom of the hill, near the creek, Bentley looked up the hill toward us, and then I saw him stop at a tree to pee. It reminded me of the day he left us and had an accident in his crate.

"Is he afraid we are going to take him home with us," I wondered. As I looked at him, I could see that Bentley WAS home. He didn't want to leave with us. Until now, a little bit of hope had remained in my heart that one day Bentley might come back to us. With a mixture of sadness and happiness, I let that hope go. I was sad that Bentley would not be coming back and happy that he was happy. I was happy that he had finally bonded with someone. I was happy that he had room to roam and a creek to play in.

Steve turned the car around, and we started back down the lane. As Bentley watched our car pass by the creek, he and the other two dogs began slowly climbing the hill in the direction of the house. He was going back home.

Marveling at what we had just witnessed, I turned to Steve and assured him, "We don't have to wonder anymore if we made the right decision for Bentley."

***

It was late afternoon on Thanksgiving Day, and I was cleaning up the kitchen, when I heard Steve answer his cell phone. It was our neighbor who had just moved away to a different subdivision a few weeks earlier. We had been neighbors for more than 20 years. He and Steve had worked on many projects together, and he was one of the two neighbors who had taken care of Buddy and Bentley, when we were gone on trips. He had even chased down Bentley on one of his break-outs. It was sad to see his family move away. He was another one of Buddy's buddies, and no doubt, Buddy missed him, too.

After he hung up the phone, Steve came into the kitchen and told me that our former neighbor had called to say he was on his way out to bring Thanksgiving Dinner to Buddy.

~~~

11 CHANGES

2013

∞∞∞

When I heard a knock at the front door on a Saturday morning in early spring, I assumed it was older kids from the neighborhood, selling products for a school fund-raiser.

Answering the door, I saw three young girls, who looked to range in age from about three to eight years, standing on the porch. I didn't know them. Standing in the grass, near the sidewalk that led to the porch, Buddy was smiling at the girl

"Can Buddy come to our house and play with us?" the older girl asked, sweetly.

Before I gave her an answer, I asked, "Where do you live?"

"We live in the house across from the street that goes around the hill," she said.

"Are the three of you sisters?"

"Yes, we're sisters," she said.

"Sure, Buddy can go to your house and play," I smiled at them.

As they turned toward Buddy, who was eagerly waiting for them, I called after them, "How do you know his name?'

Walking alongside Buddy, one of the girls called over her shoulder, "Everybody knows Buddy."

***

As the days of spring rolled by, my son's college graduation loomed closer. This spring was reminiscent of another spring that marked a milestone for him and anxieties for me. That spring was six years ago, when he had gotten his driver's license and a car. This spring, he was preparing to move an hour away from us to attend graduate school.

Friends kept telling me it was just an hour away. I knew I should be thankful he would be just an hour away, and I was also thankful to have a university in our town that allowed both kids to live at home, while completing their undergraduate studies. Still, it was hard seeing my firstborn leave the nest.

During Seth's college years, he and his friends still occasionally played basketball and football at the house. But now, instead of bicycles thrown down in the yard, his friends' cars were parked in the driveway and alongside the road. Buddy still played with them, and it was evident that these times were delightful for him.

From the time we adopted Buddy, it was always understood by the rest of us that Buddy was really Seth's dog. When the time came for Seth to move away, he mentioned that his apartment was pet-friendly, and he would like to take Buddy with him. I would have liked for Buddy to have moved with him, too, for the company and the protection.

Seth's schedule was packed with classes, internships and several part-time jobs. With no fencing at the apartment, Buddy would have had to stay inside all the time, and he would have been alone, most of the time.

Not only that, Buddy loved his home and didn't want to leave. He still only left the house once a year to go for his annual vet visit, and even then, he would balk at getting into the car. We knew that kind of move wouldn't be a happy one for Buddy.

***

After Seth moved out, I began noticing that Buddy was spending more time across the street at Seth's friend's house, lying next to the friend's car. After college graduation, this friend had bought a new car. For some reason, Buddy didn't gnaw on the tires of this car.

Late one afternoon, as I watched Buddy lying next to the friend's car, I wondered if being at the friend's house somehow made Buddy feel closer to Seth. I know, during the first weeks after the move, it was comforting to me to look out and see the friend's car there. If it was a comfort to Buddy, it didn't last long. A month after Seth's move, his friend also moved to an apartment.

~~~

12 MORE CHANGES

2014

∞∞∞

L ooking out the kitchen window, I was pleased to see signs of spring, especially leaves reappearing on the trees. In our neighborhood, all the trees do not turn green at the same time. They seemed to follow a progression of greening, beginning with the trees on the hill behind the house, then around our house and finally in the woods across the street.

My gaze turned toward Buddy playing with his soccer ball under the oak tree. This was the same soccer ball our kids had played with years ago, when their friends and Buddy joined them for games in our front yard.

The soccer ball was ragged now, with most of the covering gone. Buddy claimed ownership to the ball, now. As I watched, Buddy hit the ball with his nose and chased it down. When he tired of that, he laid down in the grass and rested one paw on the ball.

Once I had mentioned to Steve that maybe we should buy him a new soccer ball. Steve thought he preferred the old one. He was probably right. Buddy had played with this ball for years, and who knows, maybe it held memories for him.

I wondered if Buddy remembered and missed the days when our yard was filled with children, playing soccer, softball and basketball. I missed the sights and sounds of children. Our street had grown quiet — too quiet. When I took Orson for walks, I didn't see or hear children, anymore. It had been months since I had seen the three little girls who had invited Buddy to their house to play. I wasn't sure they still lived in the neighborhood.

Buddy, who had loved playing different sports with our kids and their friends, now only played soccer — alone. The basketball goal in our driveway turnaround was gone. With Seth living out-of-town, he didn't meet with friends here, anymore. Now that his friend, who had lived across the street, had moved, his basketball goal had also been taken down. And there were no more gatherings to play football at his house.

As I continued my gaze, I noticed Buddy's head would dart from side to side, keenly watching and listening to nature. He jumped up and ran to a willow oak tree, barking a few moments at robins, nestling there. Then he caught sight of a squirrel and chased it.

When Steve walked by, I murmured, "I think Buddy looks a little lonely out there."

"He still makes visits around the neighborhood," Steve responded to my observation.

"When I was walking, a woman who lives down the hill told me he visits her dog a few minutes every morning." Steve continued. "She said she gives them both a treat. And the people who just moved in across the street have met him. They were talking to me, when I was in the garden, and said Buddy visits them. They like him, too."

"He loves children so much, and I know he has to miss being around them," I said, dolefully. "I wish more children would move into the neighborhood. It's so quiet around here, now."

***

Looking out the window to see if the rain had started yet, I saw Buddy lying in the grass near the driveway. As always, he was observing all the nature activity in the yard, while watching the road for any sign of movement.

All at once, he stood up, wagging his tail and smiling. Looking in the direction of his gaze, I saw our neighbor walking up her driveway toward the road. Buddy broke into a run and met her at the end of our driveway and slowed to a walk, keeping step with her as she began her morning walk.

Buddy still had a special bond with the couple who had rescued him, years ago. Nowadays, Buddy walked mostly with the wife. When Buddy went on walks with the wife, he completed the walk. He stayed with her.

Most mornings, he would start out with Steve on his walk, go down the hill, turn around and come back to the house. Sometimes, Buddy would walk farther than down the hill with Steve, but he did not finish the walk with him.

Buddy's smile was constant as he walked along with our neighbor. He had been taking walks with her for years, since the days she took her baby along in his stroller. Her son was the one child Buddy had been around from infancy to a school-age youngster. Now that he was in school, we didn't see her son outside as much, but if Buddy caught a glimpse of him, he would make a dash to get to him.

Again, I wondered why Buddy always stayed with her during her walks. I know he loved her and enjoyed her companionship. But could it be that because she had rescued him, he wanted to protect her the way he wanted to protect us? Whether that was the reason or not, knowing Buddy, he WAS protecting her on those walks.

On this day, I was just glad that Buddy still had his walks with her to look forward to.

~ ~ ~

13 TOO MANY GOOD-BYES

2015

∞∞∞

From the kitchen window, I saw a long moving van stop at our neighbor's house across the street. Buddy was lying in his favorite spot — the front planter — enjoying a spring morning.

"Does Buddy have any inkling what this moving van means?" I wondered.

Our neighbors, the young couple who had rescued Buddy, were moving away. Steve and I had known about this move since Christmas. I felt so sorry for Buddy. This family was among the few people left in the neighborhood, who had known Buddy from his earliest days with us. Buddy's walks with the wife were, no doubt, a bright spot in his day.

Turning from the window, I thought, "This might be the best time to go over and say, 'good bye.'"

As I walked out of the garage, I saw Steve standing on the edge of the road, talking to a young man, who had with him a toddler in a stroller. I waved as I crossed the street and walked down the driveway to the young couple's house.

As I approached the house, I saw the husband and another man standing in the garage. The husband told me his wife and son had left about an hour earlier, to be at the new house, when the movers arrived. He introduced the other man as the realtor who had sold their house. Turning to the husband, I said, "We are going to miss you all. You've been great neighbors, and we'll never forget what you all did for Buddy the night he was hit by a car."

Walking back to the house, I noticed Steve was still talking to the guy with the toddler. I stopped and said, "Hello." As he introduced himself, he pointed to a house further down the street and said he lived there. In addition to the toddler, he told us he and his wife also had a child in kindergarten and were expecting their third child later in the summer.

It was good to know more children had moved into the neighborhood, especially on the day one was moving out.

I introduced him to Buddy, who was walking half circles around us, and said, "He loves children and is going to miss the little boy moving out of the house across the street."

Looking down at Buddy, I was startled to see patches of white beginning to form around each side of his nose. "Steve, look at him! Is he getting a white face?"

"He may be," said Steve, matter-of-factly. "He is almost 12 years old."

Although, I had bought Buddy an orthopedic bed, I didn't really think of him as old. He still acted like a pup most of the time, and he still chased the UPS truck around the loop. I didn't want to think about Buddy growing old.

***

Buddy ran excitedly between the two pickup trucks backed into our driveway, looking expectantly at Seth's friends as they carried boxes and pieces of furniture out of the garage and loaded them onto the trucks. As they moved back and forth from the garage, the guys kept a watchful eye on Buddy, who was trying to stay in step with them, obviously anticipating a game of basketball or football would soon be underway.

But Seth and his friends stayed on task, and soon both trucks were loaded and ready to leave for his new apartment. After finishing graduate school, Seth had been offered a job back in his hometown. He had moved in with us while he looked for an apartment. The month he had stayed with us had flown by, much like the two years he had been away at graduate school.

As we watched the trucks leave, Buddy came back and laid down in his favorite spot in the front planter. Buddy had no way of knowing that two of the guys helping with the move were now married and had other plans for the rest of the day.

The basketball goal was long gone, and the days of playing basketball in the turnaround were over. Seth's friend, who had lived across the street, was also married, and the days of playing football in his yard had ended.

But for a month, Buddy had seen Seth every day, and it had probably seemed like old times to him. It was good to have Seth back in the same town, again.

***

"Well, this is strange," I muttered to myself, as I opened an email addressed to me. "Why am I getting a job offer? I haven't applied for any jobs."

It had been more than four years since I had applied for a job. The email was from a company I had applied to five or six years ago. For two years, I had kept my application active but had never been contacted for an interview.

The email was an inquiry, asking if I was still interested in employment, with information of a part-time position available in my area. Although, I had now been retired for four and half years, I had some interest in this position, since it required only 2-8 hours per week. I assumed the hours would be worked one or two days a week.

As directed by the email, I logged into my old account with the company and applied for the position. The next day, I received another email, offering me the position with documents attached to complete and return.

Before I signed any documents, I made a call to the supervisor who had sent the emails. I asked her how the hours designated to me would be handled if I needed to be off for a family trip, specifically a family Christmas trip. She said that was no problem as the company had floaters who could cover those hours for me. With that assurance, I told her I would accept the position. That afternoon, I received another email, welcoming me to the company, along with instructions for meeting my area supervisor. That night I received another email from a woman, identifying herself as my area supervisor, setting up a time to begin work.

On the appointed day, I met with the area supervisor, who told me she would be working with me for about two weeks.

"Two positions are being filled, and you need to decide which one you want," she said. "One position will be a supervisory position, and that person will decide the hours worked by the second position."

"I didn't know that," I told her, wondering why that information was not in the email. "That doesn't really sound like a part-time job. The ad I responded to stated 2-8 hours a week. Are both positions for those hours?"

"Both positions will be for 25-30 hours a week," she replied. "Some weeks, the hours may be more than that, because there will also be some days of travel."

"I'm sorry," I told her, "but this is not what I signed up for. I also talked with a supervisor on the phone, who never mentioned anything about all these hours."

"Who did you talk to on the phone?" she asked.

I gave her the woman's name, and she said, "I don't know why she didn't tell you about the hours. This is a high-volume store, and we need someone for at least 25-30 hours weekly, and travel is required."

"I'm sorry," I countered. "My days of working 10-12 hours a day are over. I'm retired, now."

"I'm old enough for Medicare," I continued. "Actually, I've been on Medicare for a year, now."

Looking unfazed, she said the person who had previously held the position was around my age.

"If it will help you out, I can work for a week or two," I offered, "but I can't commit to all those hours."

She accepted my offer to work temporarily. As we worked together that week, she tried to persuade me to reconsider the job. She said the company was great, and the travel work was fun. Just as I started to waver, I had a flare of a physical problem I hadn't dealt with in several years. I had to consider my health.

For the past three years, I had been on a health journey that had resulted in a 40-pound weight loss and suspending two daily medications. This job would add tremendously to my stress load.

After a conversation with the supervisor, I wrote a letter of resignation to the company, expressing my appreciation for the offer and opportunity.

Afterwards I pondered, "Why did I receive this offer?

Something about that offer, and working for a week, brought a measure a healing to the rejection I had received during a futile two-year job search.

~~~

14 A SEASON OF SEASONS

2016

∞∞∞

Pouring myself another cup of coffee, I glanced outside the kitchen window in time to see two beautiful red cardinals flitting on the bare branches of a dogwood tree. Although it was a cold January morning, Buddy wanted to be outside, keeping his post, while watching the front yard and street. I was concerned about Buddy.

He didn't run anymore. It had been two months since he had raced the UPS driver. It was so sad to see him unable to run. But before I could get lost in sad thoughts, Buddy rose to his feet and headed down the driveway, smiling and wagging his tail.

Following his gaze, I saw two teenage girls walking down the street. When they reached our mailbox, Buddy was there to greet them. Both girls stopped and knelt next to Buddy and began petting him. One at a time, they then hugged and kissed him. The girls didn't seem to be in a hurry, as they both continued smiling at Buddy and loving on him.

 Does Buddy know them? Do they know Buddy? The girls came from the far end of the street, and I didn't know anyone who lived in those houses. After a few minutes, the girls were on their way, and Buddy came back to his spot.

***

Looking over the list of wedding plans, I was thankful to have two items checked off: venue and flowers. Both had been easy to book. The ceremony and reception would both take place at our church. Although some doubt had been cast on her prices, the florist of my choice had given us affordable quotes.

A year ago, Steve and I had celebrated our 25th wedding anniversary. I felt like we should celebrate this milestone, not just for ourselves but for our children, too. With both kids still in college, I had taken on all the planning and preparation of our party. I had ordered a wrist corsage and was pleasantly surprised when the florist had attached the flowers to a beautiful bracelet that I kept as a keepsake. The price for the corsage was reasonable, and I wasn't charged for the bracelet. But I had heard this florist was in demand for expensive weddings, and she was pricey.

 When I returned to her shop as the mother of the bride-to-be, I wondered if we could afford her. She immediately grasped my daughter's ideas and made suggestions that Betsy loved. When I told her, we had a tight budget, she just nodded and advised how we could stretch our dollars. We left a deposit that secured my daughter's wedding date, and the balance wasn't going to break the bank.

For the first time since Steve and I both had retired, I was stressing over money. While Betsy was finishing up her last year of college and busy with field experience, I was working on the wedding budget and plans. The third item on the wedding list had been triggering some sleepless nights. It was now February, and we didn't have a photographer booked for the wedding in July. The prices quoted by the photographers I had contacted were astronomical, some more than half my budget. When I asked about lower prices, their quotes for only two or three hours work was only slightly reduced. When I checked their galleries, I further questioned their prices. All the galleries looked the same. I knew wedding photography involved its own set of challenges in working with many people and different settings, but the prices were hard to justify.

During my years in journalism, I had worked with some outstanding and award-winning photographers, who brought an "artist's eye" to their work. Granted, some of them shunned wedding photography, but this was the kind of photography I was hoping to bring to my daughter's wedding.

By the middle of February, I was hoping to bring any kind of photographer to her wedding.

In desperation, I prayed for help in finding a photographer who was affordable. One day, my online search brought me to a Facebook page of a photographer, who was offering some specials. When I looked at her gallery, I saw a few photos depicting an "artist eye." When we met with her, I learned she was an artist. Her "special" fit right in with my budget.

Although her contract featured all the requisite wedding photos, I was convinced there would be a few ensuing from her artist's eye. I was right. She caught some "moments" at the wedding.

When budgeting for a wedding dress, without researching or shopping, I came up with a number that seemed reasonable to me. Our first trip to a store came in mid-March during Betsy's spring break from school. We gave the sales clerk our price range, and all the dresses she showed us were at the top of our budget. As I observed my daughter's face, I could see she didn't love any of them. Neither did I.

As I thought back to the days I wrote wedding stories for the paper, I remembered the list of adjectives and adverbs I would use in describing the dresses. Usually, I described the dresses in two or three paragraphs. A few dresses might get four or five paragraphs. None of the dresses my daughter had tried on ranked more than two paragraphs. The dress at the very top of our budget was a one-paragraph dress. I suggested she think about the dresses. I had photographed her in each one.

We left that shop and went to another one. At the next shop, prices were triple our budget. I made some calls to out-of-town shops, and the starting prices were not even close to our budget. It was discouraging. That evening, Betsy talked to her cousin who knew of a shop with better pricing. She said she would go with us to this shop the next day. I found the shop's Website and noticed a "red dot" sale was beginning the next day. I hoped we could find her a dress on the "red dot" rack. I also noted the store carried a certain brand my daughter admired.

A young TV personality, who had married a few months before, had worn a dress in this brand. It was a beautiful, demure wedding dress. Betsy had shown me a picture of it. We both thought it was the most beautiful wedding dress we had ever seen. For weeks, Betsy had been teasing me that I should buy her a similar wedding dress in this brand.

"I wish I could," I told her earnestly. "If I had the money, I would buy you that style dress in that brand."

"I know you can't afford to spend that much money on my dress," she consoled me. "That's okay. I'll be fine with whatever I wear. It's just for one day."

Even though she said that and meant every word of it, I knew the desire of her heart.

That night I prayed about our shopping trip the next day. My prayer was something like this: "Lord, this is my only daughter. You know how much I love her. If I was working and could afford to spend more, I would buy her the dress she wants. She will be accepting of any dress. I would love to see her in the dress she desires. I just pray that the right dress for her will be on that 'red dot' rack."

The next morning, when I awoke, a certain number was on my mind. Directing my thoughts to God, and wondering if this number was really from Him, my response was "Lord, is this the amount you want me to spend for a dress? That's too much. It's over the amount of the top of my budget."

A few minutes later, I thought, "But if I found a "red dot" dress in that brand, that amount would be an excellent price for that dress."

I decided to keep that amount in mind for the right dress.

A sales consultant met us at the entrance to the bridal store and asked about our budget. When I told her our price range, she brought out a dress at the lower end and most desirable price. It was a simple and yet lovely dress, without a train. I hadn't given any thought to a train, but all the dresses Betsy had tried on the day before had trains. She wanted a train, if possible.

The next dress brought out to us was pretty and had a short train. But it looked more appropriate for an older bride. The next dress took Betsy to "princess mode." Embellished with heavy beadwork, extending from the bodice and past the waistline, the gown's full skirt ended in a cathedral train. The sales consultant attached a tiara headpiece to a veil, completing the princess look. We all agreed on this dress. Then the sales consultant looked at the price tag, and with a crestfallen face, said, "I'm sorry. This dress was on the sale rack, but the tag doesn't have a red dot. I'll have to check the price in the computer."

She came back and said, "I'm so sorry. It's not a red dot item, but it is 20 percent off."

Even with a 20 percent discount, the dress was far above the top of my budget. It was above the number in my mind earlier that morning. We had to say, "No."

A few moments later, my niece came back with another dress. It was a dress I had passed on the rack several times, thinking it had too much beadwork for Betsy's liking. But now, she was ready to consider it. She tried the dress on, and as she turned around, I noticed something familiar about the tapered waistline. I couldn't remember where I'd seen that tapering.

The sales consultant brought out a rhinestone headband and with a few sweeping movements, fashioned Betsy's hair into a chignon, held in place with the headband. She attached a veil, edged with the same beading as the dress, to the headpiece. It was perfect.

"Betsy, this is a five-paragraph dress," I said, thoughtfully, looking in awe at my daughter, as the sales consultant and my niece nodded in approval.

"I could write another two paragraphs describing your hair, the headpiece and the veil."

And the dress had a red dot. The price of the dress, with tax, was the same as the number in my mind, earlier that morning. I told the sales consultant we would take the dress. I was happy the dress didn't need altering, and we would be leaving the store with it.

While Betsy was in the dressing room changing, the sales consultant folded the veil and put it in a bag.

Turning to me, she said, apologetically, "I know this dress is above the top of the budget you gave me, but you are getting a great price for a dress in this brand."

"What is the brand?" I asked. "I didn't see a label inside the dress."

When she told me the brand, I was stunned. It was the brand Betsy wanted. I ran back to the dressing room to tell her.

Before she put the dress back into its bag, the sales consultant said, "I need to show you why this dress is heavily discounted."

Near the back closure, she pointed to a tiny hole that had held a bead and said. "I have a bead and some thread to take with you, so you can fill the hole."

Neither my daughter, niece nor I had noticed this tiny and insignificant imperfection.

"Thank you for showing this to us, but I doubt I will be sewing back that bead," I said. One tiny missing bead didn't diminish the beauty and value of the dress in our eyes.

At home, I carefully placed the dress on a bed to look for the label. It was hidden in an encasement sewn into the back of the dress.

Still wondering about the tapering waistline, I asked Betsy to bring me the picture of the TV personality's wedding dress. I looked up Betsy's dress on the label's Website and compared the two dresses. The cut was the same for both dresses. The beading was different.

"I like the beading better on mine," declared Betsy.

"Thank you, Lord," I whispered.

***

Swinging and sipping coffee. It was a delightful combination for a break on a warm evening in June. With the wedding about three weeks away, I had started baking cookies for the cookie bar at the reception. All twenty-seven dozen cookies would be stored in the freezer until the wedding.

This was my first summer to have a swing, and I loved it. Steve and Seth, along with two of Seth's co-workers, had screened in our porch and installed the swing.

Nearby was Buddy, who had taken his favorite spot in the flower planter. Together, we listened to the sounds of children playing down the street. It was so good to hear that sound again. Two families of children were now living across the street from each other. These were young children, probably all under six years of age.

Listening to these children reminded me of my early days in this neighborhood, when most of the children played outside in the evenings. All those children had grown up and moved away. For several years, the sounds of children playing outside had been missing from our street.

Buddy's ears were perked and attuned to the squeals and laughter of the children, and his gaze was fixed in their direction. But he made no effort to join them, just as he no longer made any effort to race the UPS driver. It was difficult for him to get up and down. Although, he couldn't run and play with the children, Buddy seemed to enjoy listening to them.

Watching Buddy's health decline was difficult. He definitely had a white face, now. I wondered how much longer we would have him. I just prayed he would not go the same year Steve and I became empty-nesters.

***

Holding Orson in my arms and with Buddy by my side, I waved good-bye to my daughter and her new husband, Lawrence, as they backed out of our driveway. They were leaving to go back to their home in the city. Steve and I had kept their new puppy, Lucy, while they were on their honeymoon. They had returned this weekend for a visit and to pick up Lucy.

As I walked back into the house, I wondered what was keeping Steve. He had left nearly two hours ago to help Seth move a desk from his apartment into a house he had rented.

Just as I put Orson down on the floor, the phone rang. It was Seth.

"Mom, do you think you could come to the hospital?" he asked, in a carefully controlled voice.

"Of course, I can," I answered. "Why are you at the hospital? What happened to you?"

"It's not me," he said, his voice cracking. "It's dad. He's in ER. They think he's had a heart attack."

"I'm on my way," I told him, as I ran to get the car keys. I made a quick call to Betsy, who was still in town. They were getting gas for their car. They would be returning to the house to leave their puppy and joining me at the hospital.

In the car, I made a quick call to my brother. His wife answered and said he was out of town. I told her what I knew, and she said she would notify the rest of the family.

Then I started praying out loud in the car. I prayed all the way to the hospital. I'm so glad I did, because at the hospital, I froze with fear. I was taken to a small room with Seth, where an ER doctor met with us. She said Steve had had the heart attack after he arrived at the hospital. He had coded but seemed to be stable.

While moving the desk, Steve began experiencing severe chest pain and wanted Seth to drive him home. Thankfully, Seth decided to drive his dad to the hospital, which was less than five minutes from his apartment. The heart attack began after he was taken back to an ER exam room.

I was in shock. Steve had joined me on my health journey, about four years ago, and had done so well. He was at a healthy weight, exercised and followed a healthy eating plan.

Before Steve left ER for a heart procedure, we were allowed to see him for a moment. He was unconscious. On our way to the ICU waiting room, we followed at a distance as he was wheeled toward an elevator. At one point, two nurses threw their hands up in a halting sign, and we stopped. Later, we learned he had coded again.

When the cardiologist spoke with me in the ICU waiting room, my mind was numb. I couldn't think of any questions. I do remember thinking, "I have three children, now," because Seth, Betsy and Lawrence, my son-in-law, were all asking the doctor questions.

After the procedure was over, the cardiologist informed us that one stent had been placed in an artery, and Steve was doing well.

The children and I spent the night in the waiting room. Early the next morning, the cardiologist came back to check on Steve and told me to go home and rest.

Two days later, Steve was released from the hospital. His cardiologist said he expected Steve to make a full recovery. It was his opinion that Steve's healthy lifestyle for the past four years had probably delayed this event. Had we started earlier, it might have been prevented.

Since Steve was already following healthy eating habits, no changes were necessary in his diet. His physical activities were limited for a few weeks.

The day before the cardiac event, I had finished preparing all the garden vegetables for the freezer. We still had some vegetables to pick, so I went to the garden with Steve each morning and again in the evening. This was a welcome diversion for me.

Although Steve's prognosis was good, these were days of navigating uncharted waters. A dissonance was always there, as I knew there were still milestones to meet, especially during the first year.

One morning, that first month home from the hospital, I was sitting in the swing reading my daily Bible reading, which was in John 6 that day. In this chapter, Jesus is walking on the water and I read these verses:

"And the sea arose by reason of a great wind that blew. So when they had rowed about five and twenty or thirty furlongs, they see Jesus walking on the sea, and drawing nigh unto the ship: and they were afraid. But he saith unto them, 'It is I; be not afraid.' Then they willingly received him into the ship: and immediately the ship was at the land whither they went." John 6: 18-21

As I read these verses, I saw that the disciples were in a storm and had rowed three or four miles (five and twenty or thirty furlong) in their own strength. Steve had been in a storm. He had invested about four years in good habits before the storm of a health crisis arose. The disciples were frightened but willing to receive Jesus in their boat.

With Jesus in the boat, they were immediately at land. I wanted Jesus in our boat, and I knew Steve did, too. So that morning, I asked Jesus to get in the boat with Steve and me and to bring Steve back to health.

With our daily five-mile walks suspended for a while, Steve and I returned to walking at a slower pace and a shorter duration.

Our weekly schedule now included three days of cardiac rehab for Steve. Cardiac rehab was a blessing in many ways. Not only did the patients gain strength from the exercises, but the educational classes answered many questions I had about the heart and the medications for heart patients. It was reassuring to have nurses to talk to about questions and concerns.

An unexpected benefit was the comradery of patients and spouses. After a few weeks, these visits seemed a normal part of our routine.

***

It was the middle of October when I called our vet's office to make an appointment for Buddy.

The week before, Steve had spent four nights in the hospital for an ailment unrelated to his heart, but still undiagnosed after days of testing, including three nuclear scans. It had been a weary week for Steve, who hadn't eaten much due to all the testing, and for me, as I had only left the hospital for brief periods during the day to go home and check on Buddy and Orson

At home, I scheduled Steve's follow-up appointments, and then my thoughts turned to Buddy.

For months, I had been concerned about him. Now I had new concerns. It appeared he was losing muscle, and his bark sounded gravelly and raspy. I dreaded the appointment. What was our veterinarian going to suggest?

On the Saturday of the appointment, Lawrence, my son-in-law, went with me and carried Buddy inside. After the examination, the veterinarian gave Buddy a shot and two bottles of medicine.

"We'll see what this does for him," he said. "You'll know in just a few days if it's working. You will see him moving around a lot more. Bring him back next week for another shot. We'll give him a shot once a week for a month."

Buddy seemed more comfortable after he started the medication and began walking more. A few times, I saw him break into a short trot. I was encouraged. Maybe we can have another year with him.

Buddy didn't like taking these weekly trips to the veterinarian. Steve went with me to take him back for his third shot. Now, I was hopeful the shots and medications were working. We only had one more shot left to finish the series.

***

As we pulled into the driveway, Buddy was lying in front of the garage. We had just returned from a day trip to Betsy's home to bring her back for a dental appointment. Buddy didn't get up. That was strange. Each time, we arrived home, he still went through his routine of barking and checking out both sides of the car.

As the garage door raised up, Buddy continued to lay there. I got out of the car to check on him. "Steve, he can't get up, and his eyes are glassy!" I yelled back at him.

Getting out of the car, Steve walked over and looked at him. "He's dying," Steve said, matter-of-factly, with his eyes remaining on Buddy.

"Are you sure?" I asked, now shaking in fear.

"Yes, I'm sure. Call the vet," he said, as he got some water for Buddy.

It was late afternoon, a few minutes past 4 o'clock, but I knew the office would be open for another hour. When one of the assistants answered, she told me the veterinarian had left for the day.

When I told her, we thought Buddy was dying, she said another clinic in town accepted walk-ins, and we could try to take him there.

"If you think it's going to be soon, you can keep him there and make him comfortable," she added.

When Steve tried to lift Buddy to put him in the car, he resisted with all the strength he had left.

We made the decision right then to let him stay. Steve laid him on a rug, and we knelt next to him and kept telling him how much we loved him.

Betsy called Seth to let him know. Looking around at our neighbors' driveways, I turned to Steve and asked, "Can you tell who is home? We need to let the neighbors know, so those who want to tell him 'good bye' have the chance."

We determined that only our neighbors across the street were home. The wife had just had surgery, so we were unsure if she could come over. But we wanted her to know. Steve walked across the street to tell them. Both the husband and wife followed Steve back. When Buddy saw this couple approaching, he smiled his old smile at them.

Kneeling next to him, both began stroking his head and saying, "Buddy, we love you. You have been such a good friend. You are going to be missed so much."

"I love you, Buddy," the wife said, leaning over further to kiss him. Buddy had never looked happier. He looked completely at peace.

When I, again, said, "I love you, Buddy," he turned to look at me, smiling.

With one last look and "good bye, Buddy," our neighbors got up to leave.

 "Thank you for letting us know," said the wife. "Yes, thank you," added her husband.

"I'm glad you all were home," I told them. "Buddy was so happy to see you."

After our neighbors left, Steve and I sat down next to Buddy and watched him carefully lay one front paw over the other one. He was in peaceful repose. A few minutes later, he was gone.

Seth drove up just as Buddy passed. We stood there a few moments, looking at him. He had been with us almost 13 ½ years, but it seemed like he had always been with us.

"Buddy was a special dog," Betsy said.

"I'm so thankful this didn't happen, while we were gone," I said. "Maybe he waited on us to come home."

It was getting dark, so Steve and Seth decided to bury him the next day. I didn't want Steve to try to dig his grave, until we talked to the nurses at rehab the next morning. Steve kept saying, emphatically, "I'm going to bury him." Steve wrapped him in a comforter and laid him on a rug in the garage.

When we arrived at rehab the next morning, I stopped at the director's office and told her about Buddy and that Steve was insisting on helping with the burial.

"Yes, he needs to help," she said. "That will help him in his grief. But he should just help your son. He shouldn't do all the digging."

While Steve was exercising, I went to the waiting area and sat down next to another wife of a cardiac patient. When I couldn't stop the tears from falling or hide them behind my hands, I looked at the woman and told her why I was crying.

And she let me talk about Buddy. I talked about the days Buddy played sports with our children and their friends, his relationships with our neighbors and his declining health over the past year.

When I looked back at her, tears were streaming down her face, too.

Wiping her eyes with a tissue, she said, "I'm so glad he doesn't have to suffer this winter. The cold would have been so hard on him."

Her words were strangely comforting to me. If Buddy could have hung on through the winter, what benefit would that have been to him? Desiring to keep him longer and delay grieving over him was not what was best for him.

Later that morning, Seth and a friend helped Steve dig Buddy's grave. They buried Buddy inside the fence, where he had spent his first days with us, as a five-pound puppy.

As we stood at his grave, we prayed and thanked God for the years we had with Buddy. We offered special thanks that we were with him at his passing and knew he was happy and peaceful.

Buddy had fulfilled his purpose

~~~B~~~

EPILOGUE

After Buddy passed away, it was hard to remember a time he was not a member of our family. It was a startling realization that Steve and I had been married 13 ½ years when Buddy came to live with us, and our children were on the cusp of childhood. Now, our children were grown and gone, and Steve and I were empty-nesters. We were thankful that Orson kept the house from getting too quiet.

During those early weeks, I'd sometimes still look for Buddy when I pulled into the driveway, and then as I walked into the house, I'd quickly look away from the bottom shelf in the garage, where we had kept his treats and dog food. At night, I missed the sounds of him moving around.

When spring arrived, there was a resurgence of sadness that Buddy would no longer follow us to our vegetable garden and on our rounds, checking on the flowers. I missed hearing his bark and missed his company when it was warm enough to sit on the porch. Occasionally, Steve and I talked about getting another dog — when the time was right. But first, we were going to give ourselves time to grieve for Buddy.

About a month before the first anniversary of Buddy's passing, we felt that it was time, and in honor of Buddy, we wanted to adopt a dog that needed a home.

After praying for the right dog for us, we began our search and within two weeks, we found her — a yellow lab, about a year old. It was love at first sight...for the three of us. Yes, Orson went with us to meet her, and he loved her, too. We named her Emily.

Like Buddy, her past is unknown to us. She shares some physical similarities with him, as well as personality characteristics. She has a pointed face that is usually beaming with a smile. She looks at Orson with the same quizzical gaze that Buddy gave him, as if thinking, "What exactly are you? You sound like a dog and climb like a cat." And like Buddy, she gets along well with other dogs but seems to prefer the company of humans. Like Buddy, she is also dominant and at times docile. And like Buddy, she has a loving nature that draws people to her.

During her first week with us, as I observed Emily's remarkable social skills and intelligence, I wondered if we should pursue more than basic obedience training for her. The next week, we took her to a canine training facility, where she was evaluated by several trainers, who agreed that with her temperament and training, she could be certified as a therapy dog. Emily is now on course in her training, and once certified as a therapy dog, we hope to take her on visits to nursing homes.

We want Emily to find and live her purpose.

EMILY

Our Buddy

ABOUT THE AUTHOR

Bobbie Bruton holds a bachelor's degree in English-journalism and worked in journalism for about 12 years as an editorial assistant for the lifestyles section of a daily newspaper. In addition, she has authored articles that have appeared in regional publications. She also writes for two blogs: *A Bit of Bliss* and *Love Livin' Light*.

Buddy and his tennis ball, October 2010.

From the author…

As the first anniversary of Buddy's passing neared, I knew I wanted to do something to honor his 13 ½ years with us. My husband and I were already thinking about adopting another dog in honor of Buddy, but I wanted to do more.

One thing was certain…we wouldn't be adopting another Buddy. As my daughter put it so simply and yet so succinctly, "Buddy was a very special dog." I knew Buddy would live on in our hearts and memories. One day, I decided to put those memories on paper as a lasting memorial to Buddy and as a keepsake for our children.

As I started writing, I decided to follow Buddy's life chronologically, with each chapter of the book representing a year of his life with us. It was more than a little startling to realize Buddy came into our lives during a year of pronounced change and uncertainty. In fact, change and uncertainty remained the theme of our lives during all the years he lived with us.

It seemed appropriate and fitting to intermingle in his story the changes and challenges, facing his humans. Changes and challenges continued during our last year with Buddy. My husband and I became empty-nesters, and he survived a serious heart attack.

As I continued writing Buddy's story, I remembered that my first story published in a newspaper was a human-interest story about an endearing and quirky cocker spaniel dog. It seemed fitting that my first published book should be about a dog, a very special dog.

We waited a long time to add a dog to our family. When Buddy came into our lives, it was the right time...the perfect time.

Bobbie Bruton

Buddy in September 2016. Last picture taken of him.